IRIS MURDOCH AND THE ART OF IMAGINING

Continuum Studies in Philosophy
Series Editor: James Fieser, University of Tennessee at Martin, USA

Continuum Studies in Philosophy is a major monograph series from Continuum. The series features first-class scholarly research monographs across the whole field of philosophy. Each work makes a major contribution to the field of philosophical research.

Applying Wittgenstein – Rupert Read
Berkeley and Irish Philosophy – David Berman
Berkeley's Philosophy of Spirit – Talia Bettcher
Bertrand Russell, Language and Linguistic Theory – Keith Green
Bertrand Russell's Ethics – Michael K. Potter
Boyle on Fire – William Eaton
The Coherence of Hobbes's Leviathan – Eric Brandon
Doing Austin Justice – Wilfrid Rumble
The Early Wittgenstein on Religion – J. Mark Lazenby
F.P. Ramsey, edited by Maria J. Frapolli
Francis Bacon and the Limits of Scientific Knowledge – Dennis Desroches
Hume's Social Philosophy – Christopher Finlay
Hume's Theory of Causation – Angela Coventry
Idealist Political Philosophy – Colin Tyler
Iris Murdoch's Ethics – Megan Laverty
John Stuart Mill's Political Philosophy – John Fitzpatrick
Matthew Tindal, Freethinker – Stephen Lalor
The Philosophy of Herbert Spencer – Michael Taylor
Popper, Objectivity and the Growth of Knowledge – John H. Sceski
Rethinking Mill's Ethics – Colin Heydt
Russell's Theory of Perception – Sajahan Miah
Russell and Wittgenstein on the Nature of Judgement – Rosalind Carey
Thomas Hobbes and the Politics of Natural Philosophy – Stephen J. Finn
Thomas Reid's Ethics – William C. Davis
Wittgenstein and Gadamer – Chris Lawn
Wittgenstein and the Theory of Perception – Justin Good
Wittgenstein at his Word – Duncan Richter
Wittgenstein on Ethical Inquiry – Jeremy Wisnewski
Wittgenstein's Religious Point of View – Tim Labron

IRIS MURDOCH AND THE ART OF IMAGINING

MARIJE ALTORF

continuum

Continuum International Publishing Group
The Tower Building, 11 York Road, London SE1 7NX
80 Maiden Lane, Suite 704, New York, NY 10038

www.continuumbooks.com

British Library Cataloguing-in-Publication Data
A catalogue record for this book is available from the British Library.

ISBN-10: HB: 0-8264-9757-8
ISBN-13: HB: 978-0-8264-9757-4

Library of Congress Cataloging-in-Publication Data
Altorf, Marije.
  Iris Murdoch and the art of imagining / Marije Altorf.
    p. cm.
  Includes bibliographical references and index
  ISBN 978-0-8264-9757-4
  1. Murdoch, Iris–Criticism and interpretation. 2. Murdoch, Iris–Philosophy. 3. Murdoch,
Iris–Religion. 4. Women and literature–England–History–20th century. 5. Imagination in
literature. 6. Philosophy in literature. 7. Religion in literature. I. Title.

PR6063.U7Z53 2008
823'914–dc22
                                                                    2007048054

Typeset by Aarontype Limited, Easton, Bristol
Printed and bound in Great Britain by Biddles Ltd, King's Lynn, Norfolk

For Chel Altorf and Atie Breedveld

Contents

Acknowledgements

I wish to thank the University of Glasgow for giving me a Postgraduate Scholarship with which to pursue this research, and the Heyendaal Institute in Nijmegen for providing me with an income at the beginning and end of writing my PhD thesis. Thanks to David Jasper for his numerous comments and continuous support, and to Edith Brugmans for her careful criticisms. Thanks also to my examiners, Pamela Sue Anderson and Heather Walton, for their critical questions. I wish to thank Mariëtte Willemsen, with whom I have spent many pleasant hours working on the translation of Murdoch's *The Sovereignty of Good*. Thanks also to my postgraduate colleagues in Glasgow, especially Mark Brummitt, Darlene Bird, Angus Paddison and Karen Wenell. I wish to thank my present colleagues at Strawberry Hill for their interest in this research – Vivian Boland in particular for proof-reading the text.

My last thanks are to my partner and family. Ardo has been a constant companion, far away and nearby. I have dedicated this book to my parents, who, each in their own way, have taught me to think for myself, but never to the exclusion of others.

Different parts of this book have been published previously. I would like to thank Palgrave Macmillan for permission to republish part of my article in A. Rowe (ed.) (2006), *Iris Murdoch: A Reassessment*, pp. 175–186, Ashgate for permission to republish part of my article in D. Bird and Y. Sherwood (eds) (2005), *Bodies in Question*, pp. 147–159, and Van Gorcum for permission to use part of my article (in Dutch) in *Algemeen Nederlands Tijdschrift voor Wijsbegeerte* 96–1 (2004), 40–52.

Marije Altorf
Strawberry Hill, November 2007

Introduction

Literature and Philosophy

It is not easy to characterize the thought of Iris Murdoch in only a few lines. Murdoch left an original oeuvre, with respect to both content and form. Over a period of more than 40 years she wrote 26 novels. She was also the author of several philosophical works, including one of the first books on Sartre in the English language. This already significant and diverse number of works is complemented by several plays, an opera libretto and poems.[1]

Her unusual oeuvre has engendered a vast and diverse body of commentaries. An important and recurring question in many of these works is whether and how the literary and the philosophical works may be understood to be related.[2] At first encounter, there seems to be a strong relationship between the two. On the one hand, the characters in her novels use vocabulary taken out of her philosophical essays or they write treatises with similar titles and in a similar tone, thus suggesting that the essays provide a clue for reading the novels. So, Marcus in *The Time of the Angels* is working on a book provisionally entitled *Morality in a World Without God*. An excerpt from that work in the novel leaves little doubt that Murdoch had her own *The Sovereignty of Good* in mind (Murdoch 1966: 128). A work of the philosopher Rozanov in *The Philosopher's Pupil* is called *Nostalgia for the Particular*, which is also the title of one of Murdoch's earliest articles. Even more often, characters simply quote lines taken literally or almost literally out of her essays.[3] They also know their philosophers. Not many people would groan 'Wittgenstein' on their deathbed, but it is not all that remarkable in Murdoch's novels.[4]

In her systematic essays, on the other hand, Murdoch often writes about art and especially about literature. Art and literature play an important role in her moral philosophy. Novels, in particular a selection of novels from the nineteenth century, reveal for Murdoch what philosophical texts have much more difficulty in arguing for. Art thus indicates what an exemplary state of consciousness can be like, but also shows more common states of mind. 'Art', Murdoch argues in 'On "God" and "Good" ', 'presents the most comprehensible examples of the almost irresistible human tendency to seek consolation in fantasy and also of the effort to resist this and the vision of reality which comes with success' (Murdoch 1997: 352). Murdoch assesses in particular contemporary literature critically. She considers it 'concerned with "the human condition" ... [and not] with real individuals struggling in society' (Murdoch 1997: 291). Contemporary literature thus fails in *moral* terms and her essays on literature often end with explicit recommendations.[5]

Murdoch's oeuvre thus suggests different ways to relate the novels to the philosophical texts. It has been questioned, for example, whether Murdoch's own novels meet the standards she describes in her systematic essays. Some agree that they do, others that they don't.[6] It has also been argued that the novels are illustrative or expressive of ideas explored in the philosophical works, or that Murdoch probes her philosophical ideas in her novels.[7] By and large, it is assumed that there is some relationship between the two.

It is remarkable then that the fiercest opposition to the suggestion that her novels and her philosophical texts are in some way related has come from Murdoch herself. Most prominently in an interview with Magee she denies that the presence of philosophical ideas in her novels has any significance, baffling her readers by stating that

> I feel in myself such an absolute horror of putting theories or 'philosophical ideas' as such into my novels. I might put in things about philosophy because I happen to know about philosophy. If I knew about sailing ships I would put in sailing ships; and in a way, as a novelist, I would rather know about sailing ships than about philosophy. (Murdoch 1997: 19–20)

The presence of philosophical ideas in the novels, Murdoch suggests here, is incidental and should not be considered as a tool for interpretation of the work.

Yet, in defiance of Murdoch's own judgement, commentators have looked for philosophical ideas in the novels. Such research is often couched in terms of the question whether Murdoch was a philosophical novelist. In the first book about Murdoch's work, Byatt wonders what the notion 'philosophical novelist' means, and even 'whether it is a term of praise or abuse'.[8] Murdoch may herself feel 'horror' at being called a philosophical novelist, but this sentiment is certainly not held by all.

For Byatt's appraisal, Murdoch's criticism of Sartre is essential. Byatt notes that for Murdoch 'Sartre displays to us the structure of his own thought, but he does not give to us the *stuff* of human life', and wonders 'how far, loosely, does this critical attitude to the philosopher as novelist apply to Miss Murdoch herself?' (Byatt 1994: 209). Byatt perceptively suggests that the disparity between patterns of thought and the messiness of life is acutely felt by Murdoch, and consequently by her readers. 'A novel, she says, has *got* to have form; but she seems to feel a metaphysical regret about it' (Byatt 1994: 216–217). Yet, for Byatt, the presence of ideas in Murdoch's novels is not as intolerable a tool for interpretation as Murdoch suggests. Murdoch frowns upon the label of philosophical novelist, Byatt argues, because she objects to Sartre's didacticism. However, Byatt continues, Murdoch would not deny that her novels are structured. They start with ideas rather than characters. In other words it should not be surprising that Murdoch, as a 'practising philosopher', is considering ideas when writing novels (Byatt 1994: 210). It is this practice that has been recognized by various commentators. To read the novels with the philosophy in mind does not necessarily disagree with Murdoch's own perception of the relation between her philosophy and her novels. The difficulty starts when there is no room left for recognizing discrepancy, when the novels are read as straightforward explanation of the philosophical texts.

Yet, while the novels can arguably be read in a philosophical light, there has been, in contrast, much less debate on the possible influence of Murdoch's novel-writing on her philosophy. In the interview with Magee Murdoch not only denies the relevance of philosophy for her novels, but she also tries to save philosophy from any literary contagion. These remarks have occasioned confusion, when she argues that in contrast to literature, there is an 'ideal philosophical style'. Murdoch describes this ideal philosophical style as having 'a special unambiguous plainness and hardness about it'. It is 'an austere unselfish candid style'. Philosophers must be exact and avoid 'rhetoric and idle decoration'. Though they may use their wit at times, 'when the philosopher is as it were in the front line in relation to his problem I think he speaks with a certain cold clear recognisable voice' (Murdoch 1997: 4–5). This statement has been severely criticized by Nussbaum in *The Fragility of Goodness*. Nussbaum introduces the quotation as exemplification of the prevalent philosophical style in the Anglo-Saxon philosophical tradition. She understands Murdoch to defend a philosophical style of 'plain hard reason, pure of appeals to emotions and sense', which is 'content-neutral'. This style, however, is not at all Murdoch's, as Nussbaum acknowledges in a later text.[9]

The interview with Magee then contains curious remarks for anyone familiar with Murdoch's oeuvre. Murdoch seems to defend a style that, on consideration, is very different from her own. The misunderstanding, created by the quotation above, is partly explained by Murdoch's choice of words. Her vocabulary is surprisingly similar to that of scientific objectivity. Such vocabulary is found occasionally in Murdoch's writing. Antonaccio notes how in one of her more distinctive examples in 'On "God" and "Good"' Murdoch may also be understood to suggest an analogy between her understanding of moral realism and scientific observation. In this example Murdoch quotes Rilke, who argues that Cézanne did not paint 'I like it', but 'There it is' (Murdoch 1997: 348). Antonaccio notes that a sharp contrast between 'the artist's personal or subjective desire on the one hand ("I like it"), and the clear vision he achieves on the other ("There it is"), suggests that "reality" stands apart from the self as something wholly "impersonal"' (Antonaccio 2000: 138).

Yet, the suggestion that Murdoch is indeed supportive of a scientific approach in philosophy can only be maintained when considering such quotations in isolation. It does not last when considering Murdoch's oeuvre as a whole. Especially in her earlier writing Murdoch explicitly contrasts her interest in art and imagination with the esteem for science she detects in the philosophical writings of her contemporaries. Moreover, in her writing style, she often introduces her own voice, when for instance expressing strongly held beliefs, or continuing doubt. She also considers the use of metaphor and imagery unavoidable.[10] So, it must be assumed that in the interview with Magee, Murdoch is talking about a different kind of objectivity. She does not endorse scientific objectivity, but rather one where disregard of self is to be acquired through a long process rather than assumed at the beginning.[11] Such an unselfish style is found through exploration of personal temperament, rather than by disregarding temperament. Thus, in the opening sentence of 'On "God" and "Good"', Murdoch argues that '[t]o do philosophy is to explore one's own temperament, and yet at the same time to attempt to discover the truth' (Murdoch 1997: 337).

By calling this style 'austere' Murdoch suggests that the ability to explore in this way is not easily acquired. It should not come as a surprise then that Murdoch is reluctant to call herself a philosopher. In conversation with Le Gros she explains that she is

a teacher of philosophy and I am trained as a philosopher and I 'do' philosophy and I teach philosophy, but philosophy is fantastically difficult and I think those who attempt to write it would probably agree that there are very few moments when they rise to the level of real philosophy. One is writing about philosophy ... One is not actually doing the real thing.[12]

The 'real thing' is an austere ideal to aspire to.[13]

The remarks in this interview may also be explained by observing the rigid presuppositions in Magee's introduction and questions. The interview is part of a series called 'Men of Ideas', after the gender of all the other participants. Magee had invited Murdoch to talk about 'some of the respects in which philosophy and literature do overlap'. From the very beginning, however, Magee's firm assertions and subsequent questions ban many possible points of overlap from the conversation. He begins the interview by stating firmly at the outset that '[i]f a philosopher writes well, that's a bonus – it makes him more enticing to study, obviously, but it does nothing to make him a better philosopher'. In his first questions to Murdoch, Magee maintains a strict division between philosophy and fiction. Hence, he asks her: 'When you are writing a novel on the one hand and philosophy on the other, are you conscious that these are two radically different kinds of writing?', or he asserts: 'In your novels the sentences are opaque, in the sense that they are rich in connotation, allusion, ambiguity; whereas in your philosophical writing the sentences are transparent, because they are saying only one thing at a time' (Murdoch 1997: 3–4). So, from the outset one perceives in Magee's words the desire to ascertain a clear distinction between philosophy and literature. Philosophy is pictured as straightforward and unambiguous, whereas literature is messy and ambiguous.

These remarks by Magee evince a commonly held position that while the influence of philosophy on literature may be a matter of debate, a possible reverse influence of literature on philosophy is less often considered. This position is prominent in particular among analytical philosophers. It is therefore not accidental that the field of philosophy and literature has arisen within the Anglo-Saxon tradition. Yet, even philosophers who deliberately introduce literature into philosophical analysis do not always consider the relationship between philosophy and literature as one between equals. The prominent work of Nussbaum exemplifies this attitude. In a critical reading of her work Robert Eaglestone argues that Nussbaum engages literature as a way of expressing what cannot be said in philosophy. Philosophy thus considers literature, but only to 'help the work of philosophy'. This apprehension of literature is revealed in Nussbaum's limited recognition of the artistic aspect of literature: 'Nussbaum reads art works as people, made real through enactment and emotional involvement, but she is never able to admit that they are just art works' (Eaglestone 1997: 57; cf. Walton 2005).

Murdoch occupies a more complex position in this debate. The importance she attributes to literature also appears in her answers to Magee. These answers concur only superficially with the image of philosophy and literature delineated. Even though Murdoch replies in the affirmative to

Magee's questions and assertions, in her answers the distinction between philosophy and literature becomes more confused. She introduces, for instance, a third category of 'thinker' to accommodate 'great writers' such as Kierkegaard and Nietzsche (Murdoch 1997: 4). Thus, one may assume, for these thinkers a good writing style is more than a bonus.

Murdoch's oeuvre then raises the question of the relationship between philosophy and literature and it offers different ways to consider this relationship. Yet, her oeuvre has not only been studied because of this relationship, prominent though it may be. The importance of her work is not only or even primarily decided by the unusual combination of disciplines. Murdoch's novels and her philosophical work have been independently considered in relation to contemporary works and issues in both literature and philosophy.

The novels have created a large body of criticism, from such diverse perspectives as feminist, post-modern, and various religious ones. Byatt remarks how it is not easy to position Murdoch as a novelist. Murdoch was first associated with the 'Angry Young Men', and the character of Jake Donaghue in *Under the Net* was compared to their 'rootless picaresque heroes'. Subsequent novels showed that this classification would not do. *The Sandcastle* and *The Bell* separated Murdoch from her contemporaries.[14] Henceforth, she was regarded as a novelist in her own kind, where her yearly published novel became a phenomenon, wittily portrayed in the character of Arnold Baffin in *The Black Prince*.[15]

It does not fall within the scope of this book to provide more than a very brief overview of her novels. Of their reception I mention only one prominent characteristic, which in recent times has taken a rather peculiar form. Earlier interpretations in particular show that Murdoch must have been an imposing person when it comes to the interpretation of her work. Backus points out that the narratives of both Murdoch's 'detractors' and her 'supporters' are inadequate, precisely because of their shared starting-point 'that Murdoch's reading of her novels is critical, or at least of overwhelming importance, for their correct reading' (Backus 1986: 13). Murdoch's willingness to discuss her work, and to do so from a particular theoretical framework, must have contributed greatly to this development. Yet, even if one considers Murdoch's reading as critical (to which Backus objects in general), then it remains difficult to distil a distinct voice, for Murdoch's own criticism is full of inconsistencies, especially in the interviews.[16] It may be very natural to ask Murdoch about her own work, but it would be misleading to regard these interviews as unequivocal instruction for reading it. The interview with Magee may serve as illustration here.

Murdoch's personal concern for the criticism of her work has recently had its parallel in the attempts of some scholars to reinterpret her work from life. Conradi's biography indicative here.[17] Already in the preface to *Existentialists and Mystics* Conradi speculates on a similarity between the novels and real life: 'Is it an impertinent speculation to find something owed to Franz Stein in the gentle, scholarly and dying Peter Saward, a character in Murdoch's second published novel *The Flight from the Enchanter* (1956) ... Or in Mischa Fox, the enchanter himself, something owed to the book's dedicatee, Elias Canetti?' (Conradi 1997: xx). In his biography his tone is much more assertive, writing 'Mischa Fox/Canetti' as if the enchanter from *The Flight from the Enchanter* and Canetti are one and the same.[18] He considers this way of reading most natural, remarking in his preface to the reissue of the second edition of *The Saint and the Artist* that '[i]t is a relief to be able to report that writing her biography did not substantially change my view of the shape of Murdoch's work' (Conradi 2001a: xvii). Even if one allows for the possibility and significance of such interpretations, it is still questionable why such an interpretation would be the defining one, and have the capacity to change previously held views.

In comparison to her novels, Murdoch's philosophical writing has received considerably less attention – though this situation is changing rapidly. The difference in reception may be attributable to the unusual nature of her philosophical writing. Her philosophical career experienced an original beginning with the publication of *Sartre: Romantic Rationalist* in 1953, one year before the publication of her first novel, *Under the Net*. To write this first work on Sartre in those days was, as Mary Warnock emphasizes 'an act of genuine imagination and originality'. In the analytical philosophy of that time there was very little interest in philosophy from the continent.[19] Murdoch's interest in existentialism originated in a deep dissatisfaction with much of the analytical philosophy she encountered in Britain at the beginning of her career. Unlike many philosophers in Oxford and Cambridge in those days Murdoch was interested in moral value and concepts of consciousness. Existentialism promised a philosophical consideration of these ideas. Yet, it is not clear whether she ever considered herself an existentialist. From the very beginning of her career she was not just curious about, but also critical of the tradition.

Her second book of philosophy, *The Sovereignty of Good* from 1970, was again unconventional. At its first reception various commentators remarked on its unusual form of argumentation (see, for instance, Warnock 1971). More than thirty years later, it is regarded as an influential work in the analytical tradition.[20] This is not (yet) true of Murdoch's last and largest work of philosophy.[21] *Metaphysics as a Guide to Morals* (1992) has baffled her readers even more with its many asides, its long quotations and vast numbers of ideas and references to thinkers. Antonaccio argues that it may be best described with Murdoch's own words as 'a huge hall of reflection full of light and space and fresh air, in which ideas and intuitions can be unsystematically nurtured' (Antonaccio 1994; cf. Murdoch 1993: 422). While still working on *Metaphysics as a Guide to Morals* Murdoch suggested another description, as noted by one reviewer. The review quotes from a conversation between Crimond and Gerrard in *The Book and the Brotherhood* (1987) about the book Crimond is writing:

> 'So, it's like a very long pamphlet?'
> 'No, it's not a long simplification. It's about everything.'
> 'Everything?'
> 'Everything except Aristotle. I regard him as an unfortunate interlude, now happily over.'[22]

This quotation is not only an apt description of *Metaphysics as a Guide to Morals* as a book about everything except Aristotle, it also indicates that Murdoch was keenly aware of possible criticism of her writing. The various jokes in her novels about her philosophical work are more than just jokes. Murdoch, I would argue, was keenly aware of the limitations of the writing style and argument in her philosophical work, yet she could not express her thought differently.

Murdoch, thus, left an oeuvre that can be called original for various reasons. She wrote both novels and philosophical works, and she was one of very few authors engaged with philosophers from both the analytical tradition and the continent. Murdoch's engagement with philosophy does not fit within one particular tradition, and her philosophical works have indeed been criticized for diverting from philosophical tradition. Reviewers of Murdoch's work have argued that their expectations have not been met, and in particular *Metaphysics as a Guide to Morals* has been accused of unclear argumentation or even lack of argument. All the same, it has also been suggested that *Metaphysics as a Guide to Morals* 'might well turn out to be seen as one of the finest and most original examples of philosophy produced in twentieth-century Britain' (Mason 1996: 554). This diversity in judgement raises the question of what philosophy is and what philosophical argument is. These questions motivate the present research. It explores how Murdoch's understanding of philosophy and her attempts to form bridges between different traditions and disciplines have affected her writing style and argumentation. The next section briefly introduces the book's central argument.

'How Can We Make Ourselves Morally Better?'

The present study proposes an exposition of Murdoch's philosophical writings. It was noted that in comparison to the novels the philosophical texts have received limited attention. Whereas there are many monographs on the novels, so far only a few works attempt to situate Murdoch in contemporary philosophical debates. Of these, Antonaccio's *Picturing the Human* (2000) provides the first systematic account of *all* of Murdoch's philosophical writing.[23] The book is a remarkable achievement for different reasons. By identifying Murdoch as a 'reflexive realist' it has assembled Murdoch's scattered oeuvre into a systematic framework and placed Murdoch's thought in a contemporary debate with which Murdoch was not directly engaged. Moreover, in its methodological considerations it also provides means for reading Murdoch's unusual philosophical works.

The framework of 'reflexive realism' Antonaccio derives from the work of Schweiker.[24] Schweiker develops this framework as an intermediary position between naive realism and mere subjectivism. Reflexive realism has its starting point in consciousness, but avoids a purely subjective position by assuming the possibility of surpassing consciousness in its reflexive moments. Antonaccio uses this idea in particular when analysing Murdoch's understanding of the ontological proof. The Good that the proof is to prove does not exist 'outside consciousness as a property of things or states of affairs', Antonaccio argues. In this respect the position of reflexive realism differs from that of naive realism. The Good 'can only be apprehended through the reflexive activity of cognition' (Antonaccio 2000: 128). However, the Good that is grasped by the consciousness is not an invention of that consciousness. Instead, it surpasses consciousness as a reality that confronts the self. Reflexive realism is thus distinguished from mere subjectivism.[25] Antonaccio identifies Murdoch as such a reflexive thinker, comparing her to other reflexive thinkers, like Descartes, Kant, Taylor, and Schweiker (Antonaccio 2000: 216 n. 123 and 214 n. 27, and also 220 n. 4).

With this understanding of reflexive realism Antonaccio analyses what she considers Murdoch's most important contribution to contemporary ethics: her concern for humans in their variety, and for the individual in philosophy:

The moral philosophy of Iris Murdoch presents an important challenge to current ethical inquiry: the effort to reclaim a notion of the self as individual and to reconceive its relation to an idea of moral value or the good. Specifically, Murdoch seeks to retrieve the notion of consciousness as morally central to an account of human being and, further, to conceive

consciousness as inescapably related to the idea of the good. Such an argument is bound to be controversial in an intellectual climate characterized
by an unrelenting critique of the idea of subjectivity, as well as a suspicion
of any attempt to make substantive claims about humanity or the human
good. (Antonaccio 2000: 3)[26]

Here one encounters two groups of words that Murdoch – against the
objections of an 'intellectual climate' that has largely abandoned such
notions – seeks to retrieve and connect: self, individual and consciousness
on the one hand, and moral value and the idea of the Good on the other.

Antonaccio notes how Murdoch's concern for the individual finds its
expression to some extent in her use of 'persona'. Antonaccio speaks of 'conceptual "persona"', in quotation marks, when referring to Ordinary Language Man, Totalitarian Man, and others.[27] These personae 'represent
abstract theoretical positions in the form of identifiable human types'
(Antonaccio 2000: 23). They, Antonaccio argues, signify Murdoch's understanding of moral philosophy as 'the making of models and pictures of
what different types of men are like'.[28] She acknowledges that for Murdoch
'[m]oral philosophy needs a method appropriate to the nature of human
beings as imaginative, self-interpreting creatures'. Human beings are imaginative creatures and metaphysics for Murdoch is an act of imagination, 'not
(as some analytical philosophers would hold) a logically neutral attempt to
explain the nature of reality, but a "figurative" activity of creating myths,
concepts, and images to describe and illuminate human moral existence'
(Antonaccio 2000: 22). Yet, despite acknowledging the importance of imaginative construction for Murdoch's philosophy, Antonaccio chooses a conceptual approach to Murdoch. In *Picturing the Human* she distils from
Murdoch's scattered writings the systematic position of 'reflexive realism'.

Picturing the Human has undoubtedly made a significant contribution to
Murdoch's recognition as a philosopher. By placing Murdoch into an existing framework Antonaccio has not only translated the arguments into a systematic whole, but has also given Murdoch's work a status it has frequently
been denied. It is likened to the work of such established philosophers as
Descartes and Kant. *Picturing the Human* has also been important for the present research, especially in getting it started. Certain assumptions I now
consider mine originated in reading Antonaccio's book. This is true in particular for the importance of the ontological proof in Murdoch's philosophical thinking. Antonaccio is not the only one to attest to the importance
of this proof for Murdoch's thought, but she provides the most extensive
reading of it.

Nevertheless, points of divergence have emerged as the research progressed. In particular I question whether understanding Murdoch as a reflexive realist sufficiently acknowledges her originality and creativity. By positioning Murdoch's work within an existing framework Antonaccio has not only provided status and recognition, but also overlooked some of its original, imaginative, and comic features. By completely disregarding the literature Antonaccio in a way endorses Magee's strict distinction between philosophy and literature.

This book differs from Antonaccio in considering Murdoch's contribution to philosophy in closer relation to her interest in literature and her practice as a novelist. It argues that Murdoch is an important philosopher, *because* she has not confined herself to philosophy. In order to encompass truths from literature in her philosophical writing, it incorporates literary elements such as metaphor, imagery, and imagination. This incorporation, I argue, has significant consequences when regarding the scope and nature of her argument.

The present research starts from a question or from questions Murdoch herself poses on different occasions. I consider these the central questions of her oeuvre: 'What is a good man like? How can we make ourselves morally better? *Can* we make ourselves morally better?'[29] These are the questions, Murdoch writes in 'On "God" and "Good"', 'the philosopher should try to answer' (Murdoch 1997: 342). The addition that 'the philosopher should try to answer' these questions reveals Murdoch's assessment of contemporary philosophy. Philosophers *should* try to answer these questions yet, Murdoch would maintain, in current philosophy the questions are neither posed nor answered. On the contrary, ethics and moral philosophy have almost been forced out of philosophy (Murdoch 1997: 339). Even the few philosophers who are concerned with ethics do not ask questions about becoming morally better. Rather, their intention is to provide neutral descriptions of different forms of morality, concentrating on the notions of will and decision.

Murdoch, in contrast, considers it impossible to provide such neutral descriptions. She objects to the way in which the objective of neutrality has substantially affected the language used. At the beginning of 'The Sovereignty of Good Over Other Concepts' Murdoch argues against attempts of what she calls 'modern behaviourist philosophy' to divide metaphors into non-metaphorical components, writing 'Moral philosophy cannot avoid taking sides, and would-be neutral philosophers merely take sides surreptitiously' (Murdoch 1997: 363). She strongly objects to any attempt to neutralize moral philosophy. In different essays she persistently tries to show

how the assumed neutral views of the world are not neutral after all, but instead presume a particular set of values.[30]

Instead of aiming at neutrality, Murdoch argues, moral philosophy should do two things. First, it should provide a realistic picture of human beings and second recommend 'a worthy ideal. Ethics should not be merely an analysis of ordinary mediocre conduct, it should be a hypothesis about good conduct and about how this can be achieved.'[31] In recommending an ideal, but also in its 'realistic' picture of human beings, Murdoch's position is significantly different from that of her contemporaries. The 'realistic' picture of human beings Murdoch provides is, as she describes it herself, 'rather depressing' and could not be more removed from 'the world in which people play cricket, cook cakes, make simple decisions, remember their childhood and go to the circus' of analytical philosophy.[32] 'Selfish' is the crucial word in Murdoch's description of human beings. Human beings are selfish, concerned with their own anxieties, safety, and well-being. Choice and freedom are much smaller than is usually assumed, for in preserving itself the human psyche behaves in a rather mechanical way. The psyche spends its time in day-dreaming and in looking for consolation, 'either through imagined inflation of self or through fictions of a theological nature' (Murdoch 1997: 364). Murdoch considers this description self-evident, 'true on the evidence, whenever and wherever we look at them'. Such references to the obvious one often encounters in Murdoch's writing. Words like 'simply' or 'surely' often accompany the 'realistic picture' that philosophy should acknowledge.[33]

Murdoch refers to 'modern psychology' to sustain this understanding of the psyche. By modern psychology is mainly meant the work of Freud. Murdoch is reluctant to call herself a 'Freudian', but adopts his 'important discovery about the human mind'. This discovery Murdoch describes with the theological terms of original sin and fallen man. This 'doctrine', she admits, is not acknowledged by her contemporaries: Sartre denies it, Oxford and Cambridge ignore it, and Hampshire tries to render it harmless. Yet, for Murdoch Freud provides a realistic picture of 'the fallen man'.[34] It reaffirms her 'depressing' image of human beings. This image of human beings is not a creation of Freud, Murdoch argues, but rather one that was almost lost with the recent decline of religion. For Murdoch, Freud merely *retrieves* rather than *creates* this image. Yet, neither should it be assumed that the image is originally Christian. This insight may have been expressed by a variety of people in a variety of guises, but none is held to be original. As the bishop explains in *The Time of the Angels*: 'The outward mythology changes, the inward truth remains the same (Murdoch 1966: 101).[35]

When this is indeed the state human beings are in, it is obvious why Murdoch considers it impossible for moral philosophers to remain neutral. For to provide neutral descriptions of different forms of morality, when faced with this unfortunate state of being, is to ignore what Murdoch regards as obvious reality. To remain neutral is a moral act or decision: the decision not to get involved. Reality is (consciously) ignored and there is no attempt to, as Murdoch puts it, 'defeat the enemy', which is 'the fat relentless ego' (Murdoch 1997: 342).

Philosophers, according to Murdoch, should be engaged in this 'fight with the enemy', as she dramatically phrases it. Indeed, for Murdoch it has become all the more important for philosophers to do so, because of what she calls 'the collapse of religion'. Religion shared with moral philosophy this aim of combating the fat relentless ego and its assumed collapse makes it all the more important for moral philosophy to undertake this task (Murdoch 1997: 337). Murdoch does not substantiate her assumption that religion, and by religion is meant the Christian religion, is disappearing. She admits that the assumption 'that "there is no God" and that the influence of religion is waning rapidly' may be challenged (Murdoch 1997: 361). However, this challenge does not affect her thought, because such a challenge, she would argue, does not acquit moral philosophy of its task of considering the question of how people may become morally better. The disappearance of religion merely makes it all the more urgent for moral philosophy to do so. Murdoch is writing for a growing number of people for whom religion, in particular Christianity, no longer provides any help or direction when they look for answers to the question 'How can we make ourselves morally better?' In 'On "God" and "Good"' Murdoch refers to these people as 'those who are not religious believers' (Murdoch 1997: 344). Her own relation to Christianity she shortens to 'a neo-Christian or Buddhist Christian or Christian fellow traveller' (Murdoch 1993: 419).

Her concern for the disappearance of religion underlines both her fiction and her philosophy. From *The Bell* onwards Murdoch's literary imagination forcefully reveals this preoccupation. The novels may feature nuns, priests and even bishops who are often in doubt about their calling, but very few ordinary churchgoers. *The Bell* in particular provides a most powerful image of the situation Murdoch considers her readers to be in: an interim period, the time of the angels.[36] *The Bell* features two communities: one of nuns and another, next to the abbey, of people who belong neither to a religious order nor to the world. The latter have limited access to the abbey, only some of them are allowed to enter and then only when they are called for. This limitation is, however, in a way self-imposed. When the youngest member climbs into the convent, he imagines 'a picture of nuns fleeing from him with piercing screams and nuns leaping upon him like bacchantes' (Murdoch 1958: 178). Instead, he meets a very friendly nun, who invites him to try the swing and shows him that the door is not locked at all (Murdoch 1958: 180).

Murdoch's concern with Christian imagery in her novels has invited various responses, in particular from theologians. Jansen at the beginning of his chapter on Murdoch points out how the identification of Murdoch as a 'religious writer' is interpreted very differently. While Dipple considers religion in Murdoch's novels to have the spirituality of 'bourgeois complacency and prejudice', Ramanathan holds that Murdoch 'penetrates to the very heart of Christianity and interprets it to the contemporary world in terms which it will find acceptable', and Hawkins is surprised to find 'the strange possibility that an avowedly non-Christian writer, using Christian language and tradition for her own different ends, can produce novels of powerful and genuine Christian interpretation'.[37] Even though Murdoch may be 'an avowedly non-Christian writer', her novels can be interpreted in quite different ways, ranging from the 'spiritual' to the 'Christian'. This variety in interpretation may be understood as affirmation of the strength of her art. However, Jansen cautions against interpretations favouring one's own intention over those of the author.

Interestingly, to consider Murdoch's novels as reinterpretation of Christianity stands in sharp contrast to Murdoch's understanding of contemporary literature, expressed in different essays. In this sense she is a rather odd companion for those interested in the relation between literature and theology. Murdoch has little belief in contemporary literature. Her emphatic statement that '[f]or both the collective and the individual salvation of the human race, art is doubtless more important than philosophy, and literature most important of all' is about literature from the nineteenth century, rather than contemporary art (Murdoch 1997: 362). Of course, this general judgement allows for felicitous exceptions, and her own novels may be among them. Yet, it is the nineteenth-century novel that provides the orientation for the salvation of the human race, after the collapse of religion, and answers the question that I consider the central question of her oeuvre: 'How can we make ourselves morally better?' The answer will come in terms of an understanding of consciousness in relation to an external reality.

Thus, the collapse of religion has left philosophy with a new task, and literature is going to provide the essential orientation here. I shall argue that Murdoch's understanding of literature provides the position in her philosophical writing from which she criticizes contemporary philosophy, in particular linguistic analysis and existentialism, and which inspires her own philosophy. From incidental remarks in early essays literature develops into an intrinsic part of the argument. I shall further argue that the form of her philosophical argument changes accordingly, featuring images, imagery and metaphors, receiving its fullest expression in Murdoch's understanding of imagination and fantasy in relation to the Good.

Before I proceed to distinguish the different chapters of this book, it should be noted that the terms used above – imagination, image, imagery – are notoriously difficult to define or describe. This point is evidenced when studying imagination, and it has indeed proven to be a popular point to make at the beginning of any book or article on imagination. Thus Strawson at the beginning of an article that has inspired other works on imagination writes:

> The uses, and applications, of the terms 'image', 'imagine', 'imagination', 'imaginative', and so forth make up a very diverse and scattered family. Even this image of a family seems too definite. It would be a matter of more than difficulty exactly to define and list the family's members, let alone establish their relationships of parenthood and cousinhood. (Strawson 1971: 31)

Because it is more than difficult to define and distinguish these related words, Strawson briefly acknowledges different areas of association. He subsequently proceeds to connect two particular modes in which the word imagination is used, and thus to offer better understanding of the notion of imagination.[38]

Murdoch's understanding of imagination, image and imagery proceeds from what she assumes to be an immediate insight. Imagination is rarely described in detail, and more often introduced by urging her readers to consider – what she regards as – great art: the novels of Tolstoy, the paintings of Velasquez and Titian.[39] This understanding inspires the present preliminary understanding of imagination as a faculty of the mind, at work in particular in art and literature, but not only there. This faculty creates images, examples of which have been mentioned in this chapter, as for example in the image of human beings retrieved from Freud, or the image taken from *The Bell*. Images collectively are called imagery.

The argument of this book proceeds as follows. Chapter 2 considers the presence of imagery in philosophical discourse and more generally the often problematic relationship between philosophy and rhetoric. This chapter features a study of the work of Le Doeuff and her notion of the philosophical imaginary. The work of Le Doeuff is of importance for two reasons. It provides first a general consideration of the relationship between

philosophy and imagery, and second methodological considerations for
regarding the imagery in Murdoch's philosophical writing.

Chapter 3 examines the role of literature and in particular of character in Murdoch's earlier work. It considers the role of literature in the
confrontation with contemporary analytical and existentialist philosophy.
It thus considers Murdoch's earlier writings, from the first essays at the
beginning of the 1950s to 'The Idea of Perfection' from 1964. This last
essay also features the image of a mother M and her daughter-in-law D,
which has taken a prominent place in commentaries on Murdoch's work.
The discussion of this image in this chapter questions the extent to which
Murdoch is able to uphold an understanding of the inner life and of trans-
cendent reality.

Chapter 4 discusses the notion of imagination as in a way the successor to
Murdoch's understanding of character. It presents the distinction between
good imagination and bad fantasy and Murdoch's discussion of the notion
in Kant and Plato. By taking Kant's understanding of the aesthetic imagination out of the small corner Kant had allowed it, Murdoch presents an
epistemology in which different faculties are no longer strictly distinguished. She subsequently considers Plato's understanding of the Good not
only as the means of guiding this imagination, and distinguishing it from
fantasy, but also as a source of inspiration for high imagination.

Chapter 5 considers this notion of the Good. It argues that understanding
of this notion of the Good needs elaboration of Murdoch's concept of religion. The discussion of *Acastos* presents the particular point of view from
which Murdoch considers religion. The chapter proceeds to discuss her
interpretation of the ontological proof, wondering in particular about the
position of the fool.

The book ends with a coda: a brief reflection on the relationship between
women and philosophy. Murdoch's life received notable media coverage in
the years that I have been working on this research. Both the more serious
coverage and the sheer gossip have almost transformed Murdoch from a
thinker into an icon for Alzheimer's disease. While this book does not pretend to reverse the interest, I have felt the desire to do so. I hope it confirms
Murdoch as a thinker of great originality and importance and invites its
readers into Murdoch's work and world, which features various philosophers (except Aristotle), theologians, and novelists, as well as Oxford dons
and London artists, and which I have come to appreciate so much in the past
years. Murdoch was one of the first women who were allowed to attend university and pursue a philosophical career. In the Coda I consider if her
gender has been in any way significant for her career, as well as for the reception of her work.

Reading Murdoch

Reading Murdoch's texts can be an exhilarating and also exasperating activity. I have already noted that Murdoch's texts and in particular *Metaphysics as a Guide to Morals* are difficult to read. She refers to many different texts, from philosophy and literature to theology. Especially when first reading her texts, or when unfamiliar with Murdoch's intellectual tradition, the reader encounters various unfamiliar arguments, ideas and thinkers, which are often referred to only in passing. Understanding of these ideas and thinkers seems assumed, but it would be impossible to study all these different ideas as well as Murdoch's use of them. Even a limited study may lead one ultimately from Murdoch's writing, for the ideas and thinkers she refers to are often of great complexity. Moreover, her use of texts and ideas does not always ask for a thorough study of the thinkers and ideas she mentions.

In engaging with these texts written over a period of more than forty years, on a wide variety of topics, I have chosen to stay with Murdoch's text as much as possible. Disputable interpretations are noted, but I am more concerned with the way in which Murdoch's interpretation affects her thinking, rather than with any confrontation with another, more generally accepted, interpretation. My concern has been with the development of Murdoch's thought and I have been guided in these interpretations by what she considers important herself: literature, metaphor and imagery. The different chapters provide additional explanation of the variety of texts under consideration.

Even though I am concerned with literature and imagery I do not provide a lengthy discussion of any of Murdoch's novels, though I occasionally refer to them. I do not regard Murdoch's novels or her consideration of literature as spheres separate from the philosophical concerns. Yet, a lengthy discussion of the novels is not necessary for my research, which focuses on Murdoch's understanding of literature in her philosophical writing. Though I consider her appreciation of literature most likely to proceed from her own experience as a novelist, it would be the subject of another study to decide in what way. I refer to the novels mainly to argue the pervasiveness of certain ideas in Murdoch's thought. More importantly, this study does not aim to assess the philosophical texts in relation to the novels, as the novels have been assessed in relation to the philosophy. Rather, it intends to show that Murdoch's philosophy, as inspired by her appreciation of literature, not only makes ample use of imagery, but represents an important challenge to many suppositions about philosophy. This book will examine the presence of imagery in philosophy. Such examination may seem unusual, as it can go against the grain of the text or of ordinary interpretations. Yet, it provides insights that cannot be found otherwise, as Le Doeuff argues. The next chapter introduces her thought as inspiration for reading Murdoch's philosophy.

Philosophy and Its Imagery

Introduction

If imagination is important in Murdoch's philosophy, as this book contends, then so are philosophy's images. Philosophical argument cannot be reduced to a list of statements, but has to include imagery encountered in Murdoch's work: mother M and her daughter-in-law D, Ordinary Language Man, Totalitarian Man, the allegory of the cave, the virtuous peasant, aunties, and mothers of large families. This second chapter introduces methodology for reading such imagery in philosophical texts.

It will be essential to ask what counts as an image, and what as philosophical imagery – if there is such a thing. Philosophical texts contain obvious examples of images: those just mentioned, as well as less conspicuous ones, such as metaphors that enter texts artlessly. (Entering artlessly would be an example.) Yet, to consider not just the cave and the sun, but many other images, would change philosophical reading habits considerably and create possible difficulties. For one, it may make one too conscious of language to reflect on any ideas expressed. Such difficulties are addressed in the second part of this chapter. The third part considers the 'methodological propositions' for reading imagery in philosophy, taken from Le Doeuff's *The Philosophical Imaginary* (1989), while the fourth part explores Le Doeuff's self-image as the philosopher-fool.

The subject of the first part of this chapter may seem at first rather different from the succeeding ones. It examines Murdoch's understanding of feminism, as well as feminist interpretations of her work. By using the work of Le Doeuff, my interpretation of Murdoch's philosophical work could be labelled 'feminist', as Le Doeuff is both a philosopher and a feminist. For Le Doeuff, these two are not all that different: 'Being a feminist is also a way of integrating the fact of being a philosopher. Because for two centuries a feminist has been a woman who does not leave others to think for her' (Le Doeuff 1991: 29). Yet, the same cannot be said for Murdoch. I begin this chapter by addressing objections made against regarding Murdoch's work from a feminist perspective, partly because I find that these objections tend to come up anyway. Moreover, and more importantly, underlying such objections, as well as underlying Murdoch's understanding of feminist thinking, are presuppositions about philosophy and rhetoric central to this chapter. The most important is philosophy's understanding as a neutral investigation, which is not committed to any particular value. To argue the contrary raises several difficulties, which will be addressed throughout the chapter.

Murdoch and Feminism

It may seem immaterial to observe in a study of Murdoch's philosophy that for a long period women were not allowed to enter universities and study philosophy in an academic environment. Murdoch did not write about 'women issues', or feminism. Moreover, she was reluctant to consider her work from this perspective. And yet, she was not oblivious to feminist issues, as the few interviews in which she is questioned on the relation between her gender and her work show.[1]

Her responses present an ambivalent picture. On the one hand, Murdoch is cautious of any interpretation that would single her out as a *female* writer, rather than a *writer*. Thus, she resents questions about her preference for male narrators, about her unwillingness to consider women's issues, or about the fact that none of the women in her fiction have her strengths. She seems determined not to acknowledge any innate difference between men and women, and fiercely objects to any form of feminism that she perceives to aim for separatism: 'The point of liberation is not, and this is to differ with certain views of women's lib, to say we're better, or we're special, or we're wonderful, but just to be equal, to be ordinary, to join the human race, to be people, just people like everybody else' (Dooley 2003: 83). Yet, these interviews demonstrate, on the other hand, Murdoch's awareness of persistent sexual inequality. To Hobson she argues that women's emancipation is only starting; to Heusel she says, '[u]nfortunately, it's still a man's world. A man doesn't have to explain what it's like to be a man but a woman has to explain what it's like to be a woman.'[2] Murdoch approves of women's liberation as far as it seeks to discard these distinctions, and the most important tool for achieving this equality, she repeatedly stresses, is education.

Implicit in these remarks is a distinctive understanding of what it is to be *ordinary*. As Margaret Moan Rowe puts it:

> Murdoch asserts that men and women are the same ... Then she goes
> on to suggest there is a great difference: somehow men are already

there. Their presence defines the human race. Women have to join the human race and a principal route to that connection is education. (Rowe 2004: 80)

Murdoch endorses feminism that seeks social and political reforms. Yet, she keeps this form of women's liberation strictly separate from the world of literature and philosophy, which are in a realm where gender does not play a part.

This position raises problems for feminist interpretations of Murdoch's work, because for those this separation cannot hold. Feminist interpretations of works of literature or philosophy can be very different. Yet, they all start from the assumption that social, cultural, or natural differences between men and women are reflected in literary and philosophical writing. This starting-point endorses the examination of texts from the point of view of the depiction of gender, or of gender-related partiality towards a certain writing style or certain topics. Yet such an approach needs justification when an author refuses to address gender issues and is even averse to singling out women's problems. And when the author has significantly influenced the interpretation of her work – as Murdoch has – the interpreter needs some courage as well.[3]

It is not surprising then that feminist interpretations of Murdoch's novels had a cautious start. In 1993 Griffin finds only a few critical studies on Murdoch that consider gender. Of the four authors Griffin discusses – Goshgarian (1972), Cohan (1982), Seiler-Franklin (1979) and Johnson (1987) – the last most significantly illustrates how Murdoch's position has shaped interpretation of the novels. Johnson almost apologizes for reading Murdoch's novels through feminist theory. In what she calls her 'short' or 'very short' book she acknowledges that to place Murdoch in a feminist debate ignores Murdoch's stated position. Both the modest length of the work and the different perspective create Johnson's misgivings. She expects her approach to appear 'partial and *eccentric*', and admits to 'being particularly anxious to avoid what might be construed as a "narrowly feminist" reading' (Johnson 1987: xi). However, it is not clear what Johnson's misgivings are. Griffin wonders why Johnson 'was "particularly anxious to avoid", who she assumes would "construe", and what she takes to be a "narrowly feminist" reading' (Griffin 1993: 12). Would Johnson have had similar misgivings if her approach had been equally un-Murdochian yet not feminist? Does she think that feminist readings *as such* are more likely to be narrow, or that a feminist reading *of Murdoch's work in particular* is more vulnerable to such criticism? Yet, Johnson's qualms are not isolated. They reflect generally held assumptions by (feminist) critics concerning Murdoch's work.

However, despite this cautious start, there is now a growing body of research into the role of gender in Murdoch's novels.[4] Her philosophical texts, by contrast, have not yet received the same amount of attention from feminist thinkers. Those texts present themselves as even less obvious objects for such attention than the novels.[5] Again, Murdoch's own remarks as well as the existing body of interpretation may have defused any project at its start. Murdoch's reading of *The Second Sex* could, for instance, have been a potentially interesting research project. Murdoch is known to have appreciated this feminist classic, and yet there is little to suggest any connection with her own work. Quoting from a letter to Raymond Queneau, Conradi mentions that she believed the book's ' "fierce war-like manner" fifty years ahead of its time' (Conradi 2001b: 309). But this tantalizing remark raises more questions than it answers. Murdoch herself suggests in an interview that *The Second Sex* has had a profound influence on her, but she carefully describes her admiration for de Beauvoir in terms of a *personal* relationship. To Hale she says, 'Simone de Beauvoir is someone I admire enormously. *The Second Sex* is a very good book and makes me like her as a *person*, although I've never met her.'[6]

When studying her philosophy it is easy to forget that Murdoch was one of the first women to study and teach philosophy at a university. It may thus come as a surprise that she even experienced some of the past's regulated inequality when she was at Cambridge. The University did not grant degrees to women until 1948. Murdoch was there a year before (Conradi 2001b: 261, 633 n.1). In the year that Murdoch went to Oxford, Virginia Woolf published *Three Guineas*, and still Murdoch can confess to being 'not very much interested in the female predicament' (Dooley 2003: 61). Instead, she maintains: 'I have never felt picked out in an intellectual sense because I am a woman; these distinctions are not made at Oxford' (Dooley 2003: 32).

Such indifference may of course indicate an important achievement in the feminist endeavour to create equality, and Murdoch seems to suggest that she and her contemporaries were no longer singled out for being women. When Murdoch began her philosophical career, Oxford and Cambridge employed a number of prominent female philosophers – friends and colleagues of Murdoch. With Elizabeth Anscombe, Murdoch shared a passion for the work of Wittgenstein and she dedicated *Metaphysics as a Guide to Morals* to her. Mary Midgley and Philippa Foot were life-long friends. Mary Warnock entered Oxford only a few years later (Conradi 2001b: *passim*; Warnock 2000: 39ff.). Until the recent appearance of two autobiographies by Midgley and Warnock, none of these women had addressed their novel existence as a female philosopher employed by a university.

They must have been aware of the novelty of their positions, but they did not feel the need to make it the subject of academic scrutiny. Being a female philosopher does not, of course, obligate one to comment on the relationship between women and philosophy, or to be a feminist. Given the fact that most feminists are women it is more likely, but certainly not necessary. The subject of 'woman' is, and has been, as de Beauvoir argues, often 'irritating, especially to women' (De Beauvoir 1997: 13). Ignoring the novelty of one's position can, moreover, occasion a situation in which it becomes more ordinary. For those women, having access to education was the great achievement. After that, there was little left but to persist.

However, I would argue, it is worthwhile to consider the exceptional position of this group of female scholars, if only to explain why more than fifty years later philosophy departments still employ comparatively few women. In recent years it has become more widely recognized that the practice and nature of philosophy are not always hospitable to women or members of other minority groups who have only recently had access to universities. Feminists would argue that the practice and content of almost all professions contain means of excluding women, and philosophy is no exception. Yet philosophers seem more reluctant to consider this suggestion than scholars in other disciplines. The reason for this reluctance may be found in presuppositions implied in the understanding of both philosophy and feminism, and are evident in the writings of two of Murdoch's contemporaries, Midgley and Warnock, on the few occasions when they consider the topic of 'women and philosophy'.

In her recently published memoirs, *The Owl of Minerva* (2005), Midgley considers why she, Anscombe, Murdoch, Foot and Warnock 'all made [their] names in philosophy' and comments on the exceptionally large number of women in Oxford when she was a student. Most men, she observes, were fighting in the Second World War and their absence had important consequences for the future academic careers of these women:

> The effect was to make it a great deal easier for a woman to be heard in discussion than it is in normal times . . . Sheer loudness of voice has a lot to do with the difficulty, but there is also a temperamental difference about confidence in the amount of work that one thinks is needed to make one's opinion worth hearing. (Midgley 2005: 123)

Having found their voices, Midgley continues, all of them went on to challenge the prevalent understanding of ethics, which was inspired by logical positivism (Midgley 2005: 123–124).[7]

In her *A Memoir: People and Places* (2000) Warnock also expresses regard for Foot, Anscombe and Murdoch – all 'remarkable and original women' –

and wonders 'whether their originality had anything to do with gender'. She
suggests that 'women are less prone to jump on bandwagons than at least
some of their male colleagues, are also and more reluctant to abandon
common sense' (Warnock 2000: 39). Again, the women are praised for
their independence of mind, but unfortunately Warnock does not pursue
the relation between common sense and good philosophy.

One would certainly have expected Warnock to address the relationship
between women and philosophy in her earlier collection of essays by women
philosophers (1996). However, even here she appears surprisingly reluctant
to consider the possibility that there would be anything different to say
about 'women and philosophy' than there is about 'men and philosophy'.
She effectively refuses to consider any possible reason for compiling this collection. The reason for this refusal becomes apparent, when she explains
why she has included only a few feminist texts. While Warnock admits that
much of what is written on 'the Women Question' would satisfy her 'criteria
of generality and of the hoped-for explanation of phenomena', Warnock
finds 'too much unexamined dogma in these writings, too much ill-con-
cealed proselytizing, too little objective analysis, to allow them to qualify
for inclusion among philosophical writing proper' (Warnock 1996: xxxiii).
Like Murdoch, Warnock understands that philosophy 'must be concerned
with "us" in the sense in which "we" are all humans. The truths which philosophers seek must aim to be not merely generally, but objectively, even
universally, true. Essentially, they must be gender-indifferent' (Warnock
1996: xxxiv).

Warnock's dislike of dogma and her decision to include only writing
that is 'universal' would find support from many philosophers. However, support does not entail practice. Warnock appears unaware that this
criterion, used strictly, would exclude many prominent works from the philosophical canon. Philosophical texts too often consider only a privileged
group, and thus are not 'concerned with "us" in the sense in which "we"
are all humans'. Warnock's collection suffers from a contradiction in its
conception: on the one hand, she has selected texts by women philosophers
only, and it cannot have escaped her that there is no need for such a selection of essays by men. On the other hand, the possibility that this difference
may be to do with 'women and philosophy' is repudiated from the beginning: the text on the cover states that the 'great subjects of philosophy . . .
are arguably gender indifferent since the search for truth is objective'.
Warnock recognizes that female and male philosophers are not equal in all
respects, but a strong belief in philosophy's claimed universality prevents
her from exploring whether any such differences may be significant for
doing philosophy.

This contradiction is endorsed in Warnock's conclusion, where she finds that despite the omission of specifically feminist authors from her anthology, a disproportionate number of texts are concerned with moral or political philosophy, and as such recall the view of the 1950s and 1960s 'that moral philosophy was a woman's subject, a kind of soft option' (Warnock 1996: xlv). Warnock hastens to add that this is not the only field in which women philosophers have been successful. She concludes, '[i]n the end, I have not found any clear "voice" shared by women philosophers ... they turn out, unsurprisingly, to be as various as their male colleagues. I believe this a matter not for disappointment but for pride' (Warnock 1996: xlvii).

So, neither Midgley nor Warnock considers gender to be of any *philosophical* significance. They do allow for some points of similarity among female philosophers: Midgley notices a shared opposition to the understanding of ethics prevalent in logical positivism, and Warnock finds that many of the texts by female philosophers are concerned with either moral or political philosophy. It is acknowledged that the practice of philosophy can be difficult for women, when their voices and temperaments make them less likely to be heard. Yet, none of these difficulties is related to their understanding of philosophy, or more particularly of good philosophy. For Midgley and Warnock, philosophy is gender-neutral.

This idea that philosophy is gender-neutral is still current, despite being increasingly an object of feminist criticism. It is also still defended with the zest shown by Warnock. Philosophers are reluctant even to *consider* the possibility that gender inequality, which over the centuries has been prevalent in almost every aspect of society, has also affected philosophy. In 'Is the Feminist Critique of Reason Rational?' (1995) Alcoff convincingly argues why this is so. Her landmark essay is a response to appeals by Nussbaum and Lovibond to keep feminism and philosophy separate. In particular Nussbaum presents the discussion as one with only two alternatives: either one holds philosophical reasoning to be universal, or one abandons reason and in doing so loses the means to claim equality. Not surprisingly, Nussbaum strongly endorses the first possibility. She explicitly expresses the fear that the intrusion of feminism into philosophy jeopardizes feminism's project. By questioning reason's universality, feminism risks a return to those days when women were restricted in the roles they could play. Again, women are to be excluded from philosophy, only this time by radical feminism rather than by the authorities within a patriarchal society.[8]

Alcoff counters these arguments by maintaining on the one hand that philosophy is not as universal as Nussbaum assumes, and on the other that any feminist challenge to reason does not necessarily lead to irrationality. In other words, the relation between philosophy and feminism does not need to be put in Nussbaum's absolute terms: there are more possibilities than the alternatives suggested. This becomes particularly clear when considering the various misogynistic remarks found in philosophical texts. Female philosophers have had to engage with texts that deny them the ability to think rationally.[9] While it has been argued that the misogynistic excerpts are merely incidental slips, or that they reflect the mores of the time, Alcoff doubts this conclusion. She considers the disparity between misogyny and philosophy's alliance to truth as too significant. Philosophers cannot claim to pursue the truth and at the same time tell blatant lies about women.

To say as much is stating the obvious, and yet it is difficult to accept. For it affects philosophy at its core – at its identity, or what Le Doeuff calls its 'shameful face' (Le Doeuff 1989: 1–20). Philosophers have always found it difficult to define their discipline, and yet esteem for their subject, or perhaps for themselves, made them state clearly what it is not. Philosophy has often been defined in opposition to rhetoric, to appeals to emotion, to the use of beautiful instead of logically sound arguments, or to hidden ideologies (Alcoff 1995: 69; Le Doeuff 1989: 1). Rhetoric has traditionally been considered at best superfluous, and at worst misleading. Thus to argue that rhetorical quips about old women or faithful wives are part of the philosophical argument undermines philosophy's legitimacy.[10] This creates the anxiety that has singled out feminist philosophy for the criticism of being irrational. Yet, as Alcoff points out, feminist philosophy is not alone in challenging reason. It is a general, philosophical activity (Alcoff 1995: 68–69).

Thus Alcoff pleads for philosophy 'to become more rhetorically self-conscious' and she introduces a 'dialogical model of truth' where the relationship between philosopher and subject is not a 'positivistic' one, 'in which an active knowing agent confronts a passive object', but rather 'a conversation between participants' (Alcoff 1995: 70ff.). She concludes that if 'truth is understood as the product of an argument (involving two or more participants), then all the contributing elements of that argument need to be analysed within an epistemological characterisation of its results' (Alcoff 1995: 71). The imagery, metaphors and myths of a philosophical text are part of this conversation and Alcoff at this point endorses the work of Le Doeuff.

This emphasis on the dialogical character is one that fits Murdoch's work well. Murdoch wrote dialogues, texts properly deserving this title, as well as many conversations between fictional characters in her novels. It has also been argued that her philosophical writing in general and *Metaphysics as a Guide to Morals* in particular is best described as having a dialogical or mime-like character (see especially Tracy 1996: 54–75). Murdoch then occupies a complex position in between the two extremes discussed. When asked in interviews she argues that because she is concerned with 'things on the whole' her main characters are males. When thus considering her novels Murdoch equates the male with the universal position to which women need to aspire.[11] She similarly maintains that in the philosophical world of Oxford she is not singled out for being a woman, because 'these distinctions are not made'. Yet, in her philosophical writing she exposes the assumed neutrality of arguments and considers imagery and other rhetorical devices a valid part of philosophy. Thus, like many philosophers, Murdoch seems imbued with anxiety about the split between philosophy and rhetoric. When questioned in interviews about aspects relating to this split, her arguments are confusing rather than elucidating in relation to her own writing. Most importantly, the interviews have deflected her readers from the obvious similarities between Murdoch's philosophy and some feminist interpretations, most importantly an understanding of philosophy as neutral. It is these similarities that endorse my feminist reading.

Metaphors, Images and Pictures

Images and imagery are important in Murdoch's philosophy. To claim as much may suggest that one has a clear understanding of these notions. Any study of imagery and imagination in philosophical texts may be expected to define these concepts at its start. However, neither Murdoch nor Le Doeuff commences their work by decisively answering the questions of what images are, or what imagination is. Understanding of these notions is rather found through examples and through a discussion of the significance of particular images in philosophical texts.

It should be noted that Murdoch and Le Doeuff not only leave out a definition of imagery, but also avoid the perennial question 'what is philosophy?' Instead, they uphold their positions as philosophers by, for instance, finding themselves worthy companions: Le Doeuff claims that the Shakespearean fools she wanted to be when she was a child 'were the distant heirs of Socrates' and Plato is for Murdoch 'the philosopher under whose banner [she is] fighting' (Le Doeuff 1991: 9; Murdoch 1997: 364). Yet, even if they are excused for not defining philosophy – and they are certainly not the only philosophers to shy away from this question – a definition of images and imagery might still have been expected. However, with respect to the work of Murdoch and Le Doeuff, this expectation has to be adjusted.

In the opening lines of 'The Sovereignty of Good Over Other Concepts', Murdoch most explicitly maintains that the use of images and metaphors is neither marginal nor accidental and that philosophy cannot and should not avoid using these. The text opens forcefully. Metaphors, Murdoch maintains, are not just decorations, but 'fundamental forms of our awareness of our condition'. Philosophy in the past recognized their importance and 'concerned itself with what it took to be our most important images, clarifying existing ones and developing new ones'. Yet, Murdoch points out, this practice is no longer common, because '[p]hilosophical argument which consists of such image-play, I mean the great metaphysical systems, is usually inconclusive, and is regarded by many contemporary thinkers as valueless' (Murdoch 1997: 363). Murdoch's argument here is directed against efforts by 'modern behaviouristic philosophy' to remove the use of metaphorical language from philosophy – efforts still made today. Such efforts are, Murdoch argues, motivated by the desire to make philosophy neutral. She holds, in contrast, that moral philosophy 'cannot avoid taking sides, and would-be neutral philosophers merely take sides surreptitiously' (Murdoch 1997: 363). What these philosophers fail to see, according to Murdoch, is that metaphors are not mere decoration, but 'fundamental forms of our awareness of our condition'. Thus, at the very beginning of Murdoch's essay, the importance of imagery and metaphors for philosophy is maintained, and the notions of metaphor and image are introduced. Yet, Murdoch never provides an explicit distinction between or explanation of these notions.

What metaphors are is to be deduced from the quotation above and the examples given throughout the essay. In the quotation above she argues that metaphors make one aware of one's condition, and that it is impossible to discuss certain concepts without using metaphors. She indicates three possible forms: 'metaphors of space, metaphors of movement, metaphors of vision'. Later on in the same essay she reflects on the metaphor of the Good and the sun, which she deems the most important of all (Murdoch 1997: 377ff.). Murdoch also mentions Love as a metaphor (Murdoch 1997: 384). So, the Good, the sun and Love are all examples of metaphors. Murdoch understands these in their original meaning of *meta-ferein*, that is *trans-ferring* a literal meaning to something else, which can't be described literally. Object and events are perceived *as* this or that. '"Seeing as" is everywhere and it is the stuff of metaphors.'[12] 'Our condition' understood as moral pilgrimage can only be described in such metaphors, where the Good is a form of perfection that does not have its equivalent in this world (Murdoch 1997: 374ff.).

In the same passage the Good and the sun are also called *image* and *picture*. The frequent appearance of these words throughout the essay emphasizes how Murdoch naturally thinks in imagery. She uses imagery not just in pursuing her own thought, but also to describe, for instance, Kant's philosophy, as well as contemporary ethics, and its 'stern picture of solitary all-responsible man' (Murdoch 1997: 366). It is this characteristic of Murdoch's thought that Antonaccio captures in the title of her book *Picturing the Human* (2000). The book takes its cue from Murdoch's description of moral philosophy: 'Man is a creature who makes pictures of himself and then comes to resemble the picture. This is the process which moral philosophy must attempt to describe and analyse' (Murdoch 1997: 75; cf. Antonaccio 2000: 44). Philosophy for Murdoch, Antonaccio argues, is a form of picturing. A prominent picture she considers is that of the mother M and her daughter-in-law D from 'The Idea of Perfection' (Antonaccio 2000: 22; cf. 87–95).

Are pictures and images the same as metaphors? Do they also express a truth that cannot be translated into non-metaphorical language? These questions cannot be readily answered. Murdoch's free use of the terms seems to suggest as much, but this has not always been acknowledged by commentators.[13] Moreover, the list of imagery is far from exhausted. 'Solitary all-responsible man', M and D, the Good, the sun and Love have all been recognized as metaphors or images. Yet, Murdoch's essays are full of yet more imagery that has not been recognized as such. Take, for example, the battle-like metaphors in 'On "God" and "Good"', where Murdoch treats the history of philosophy as a chronicler. 'To do philosophy is to *explore* one's own temperament, and yet at the same time to attempt to *discover* the truth.' Present-day philosophers, however, are experiencing hard times, because '[a]reas peripheral to philosophy expand ... or collapse', and the proper heir, existentialism, is degenerated, yet still capable of ... 'getting into the minds of those ... who have not sought it and may even be unconscious of its presence' (Murdoch 1997: 337–338, emphases added). Battle is everywhere: 'Wittgenstein had attacked the idea of the Cartesian ego or substantial self and Ryle and others had developed the attack' (Murdoch 1997: 339). And: 'determinism as a total philosophical theory is not the enemy ... In the moral life the enemy is the fat relentless ego' (Murdoch 1997: 342). Many curious images can be added to this more violent imagery. In 'The Sovereignty of Good Over Other Concepts' Murdoch wonders what 'place is left in this stern picture of solitary all-responsible man for the life of the emotions'. Her reply: the emotions 'enter through a back door left open by Kant and the whole Romantic movement has followed after' (Murdoch 1997: 366). The logistics are puzzling. Does the Romantic movement follow the emotions through the same back door, or does it follow Kant in leaving the back door open? Or what to think of the portrayal of contemporary philosophy as 'a happy and fruitful marriage of Kantian liberalism with

Wittgensteinian logic solemnised by Freud' (Murdoch 1997: 305–306)?
Remembering the various marriages in Murdoch's novels certainly adds a
sense of doom.[14]

It is clear that Murdoch's philosophical writing does not at all correspond
to Magee's description in the 1978 interview. In Chapter 1 I argued that
Magee starts the interview by firmly distinguishing between philosophy
and literature, with which he cuts short the discussion on the relation
between the two. Magee holds that the sentences in Murdoch's philosophical writings and in her novels are very different. The former are 'transparent, because they are saying only one thing at a time'. The latter are
'opaque, in the sense that they are rich in connotation, allusion, ambiguity'
(Murdoch 1997: 4). This distinction clearly does not hold. Murdoch's philosophical texts better fit Magee's description of the language in her novels.
The similarities between her philosophical and literary works are indeed
striking.[15] As in her novels, the story of her philosophy features various
unpredictable heirs and happy marriages facing a rocky period. When
back doors are left open, there is no telling who will enter.

Yet, Murdoch's philosophical texts are no novels, and it is necessary to
find a way to consider these various images philosophically. Murdoch does
not naively assume language to simply denote reality. Already in *Sartre:
Romantic Rationalist* she notes:

> We can no longer take language for granted as a medium of communica-
> tion. Its transparency has gone. We are like people who for a long time
> looked out of a window without noticing the glass – and then one day
> began to notice this too. (Murdoch 1999: 64)

It would not do to assume a straightforward meaning to her philosophical
writing. However, neither could one assume that Murdoch follows
Nietzsche here, and maintain that metaphors do not correspond to originals
at all, nor attribute to Murdoch a post-modern understanding of meaning as
infinite deferral (cf. Nietzsche 1988a; Jansen 2001). Murdoch's writing
does not exhibit the self-conscious style that usually accompanies this
understanding.

Murdoch's writing steers away from this stark choice between 'none is
metaphor' and 'all is metaphor', as can be shown by reading her work
through Le Doeuff's notion of the *philosophical imaginary*. Like Murdoch,
Le Doeuff also refrains from any definition of imagery. Instead, she provides a long list. Arguing at the beginning of *The Philosophical Imaginary* that
'philosophical discourse is inscribed, and declares its status as philosophy
through a break with myth, fable, the poetic, the domain of the image',

Le Doeuff notes that nevertheless one finds in philosophical texts 'statues that breathe the scent of roses, comedies, tragedies, architects, foundations, dwellings, doors and windows, sand, navigators, various musical instruments, islands, clocks, horses, donkeys and even a lion, representatives of every craft and trade, scenes of sea and storm, forests and trees' (Le Doeuff 1989: 1). The absence of any general description is deliberate here. Le Doeuff does not explain the absence immediately, but later notes, for instance, that such a description may make one disregard that '[t]here is not one *reason*, or one *imaginary*' (Le Doeuff 1989: 5). More importantly, for Le Doeuff, imagery is connected to the question of philosophical reasoning. What counts as imagery in a particular philosophical text is also decided by the reasoning of that text. Therefore, what is and what is not an image cannot be decided in general terms, or prior to the reading of any particular text. Using imagery, or disapproving of such use in philosophical texts, is not just engaging in an argument about stylistic means within such texts. Rather, Le Doeuff argues, such use or disapproval arises from values underlying the thought. These values often concern the nature or status of philosophical reasoning and of philosophy. The notion of the philosophical imaginary signifies this kind of enquiry (Le Doeuff 1989: 3).

With the term 'imaginary' another member of what Strawson characterized as 'a diverse and scattered family' of terms is introduced. Chapter 1 argued that the terms imagination, image and imagery are part of an extensive family of related terms. These terms were said to be notoriously difficult to define or describe and the relationship of one to another best understood from careful examination. A preliminary understanding of imagination and image I retrieved from what Murdoch considers an immediate understanding of these terms obtained from considering art. The term 'imaginary', however, cannot be treated in quite the same way, because rather than having many uses, it has one central meaning in feminist thinking, most prominently in the work of Irigaray. Le Doeuff's use of imaginary, however, is different from Irigaray's.[16]

In this context it is illuminating to repeat the argument put forward by Anderson, in *A Feminist Philosophy of Religion*, where she maintains 'a critical distinction between Le Doeuff's philosophical imaginary and Irigaray's male imaginary'. Quoting Grosz, Anderson argues that Le Doeuff 'distinguishes her [philosophical] notion sharply from Lacan's. It is not a psychological term describing the narcissistic and identificatory structure of two-person relations; rather, it is a rhetorical term which refers to the use of figures of imagery in philosophical and other texts' (Grosz 1989: xviii–xix, as quoted in Anderson 1998: 210). Le Doeuff's notion of the philosophical imaginary is, thus, a rhetorical term. Consequently, Le Doeuff proposes with her notion of the philosophical imaginary a form of research into philosophy's rhetoric and the specific use particular texts make of imagery. The imagery under scrutiny is not necessarily found in any collection of images known. Instead, imagery can be anything from Le Doeuff's concern with 'woman' to Murdoch's understanding of literary character and examples of analytical imagery discussed by La Caze (La Caze 2000 and 2002). What is or is not imagery is not decided in advance, but by the argument presented in a particular text.

The notion of the philosophical imaginary introduces a strong connection between imagery and argument. Such a connection between imagery and argument is only suggested by Murdoch when she writes that '[p]hilosophical argument which consists of such image-play ... is usually inconclusive, and is regarded by many contemporary thinkers as valueless'. Is one justified to discern a causal relationship? Is it that because this image-play, which needs metaphors, is inconclusive, it is regarded as valueless? Le Doeuff would be more assertive. Yet both thinkers agree on the importance of imagery and are constantly questioning what philosophy is and should be about.[17] The examination of imagery cannot ignore these questions.

The Philosophical Imaginary: Methodological Propositions

Le Doeuff thus provides the necessary 'methodological propositions', taken from the introduction to *The Philosophical Imaginary*, for reading imagery in philosophy. These propositions should not, however, be understood to 'encapsulate a method systematically deployed but are rather a concluding appraisal designed to help outline a programme for further work' (Le Doeuff 1989: 7). Indeed, neither in these essays nor in later work should one expect Le Doeuff to follow these propositions exactly. This should not be regarded as an omission but rather, as will become apparent, as an intrinsic element of her thought.[18]

The methodological propositions are written after the different essays that make up *The Philosophical Imaginary*. This notion of philosophical imaginary designates a particular approach Le Doeuff developed while working on these essays. She started her work on the different essays not with this notion or methodological propositions, but with different hypotheses about 'the functioning of imagery in texts when its presence is supposedly abnormal'. The use of imagery signifies the difficulties of a text. Imagery can either justify what cannot be justified otherwise, or it can work against the arguments provided (Le Doeuff 1989: 3). In either case, images cannot be dismissed without change in content.

Images are then a substantial part of philosophy, yet, Le Doeuff maintains, this has seldom been acknowledged in the history of philosophy. Her argument here has inspired that of Alcoff, discussed earlier. Philosophy has affiliated itself with 'the rational, the concept, the argued, the logical, the abstract', Le Doeuff writes in the first paragraph of her preface. Even if philosophers have avoided such an affirmative statement they have been decisive about what philosophy is not. 'Philosophy is not a story, not a pictorial description, not a work of literature. Philosophical discourse is inscribed and declares its status as philosophy through a break with myth, fable, the poetic, the domain of the image' (Le Doeuff 1989: 1). To maintain then that 'imagery is inseparable from the difficulties, the sensitive points of an intellectual venture', or that 'the meaning conveyed by images works both for and against the system that deploys them' goes beyond assumptions of even those philosophers for whom 'thinking in images' has become acceptable.[19] And yet, Le Doeuff maintains not just that images are a suitable topic for philosophy, but that they form an essential part of philosophical discourse.

For the analysis of such imagery Le Doeuff distinguishes four stages: denegation, iconographic investigation, erudition and structural analysis.[20] The division into these stages reads as a rhetorical device. Philosophy, it was argued earlier, as a discipline has almost always denied its own rhetoric. In contrast, Le Doeuff maintains not just that philosophy uses rhetoric, but even that it has developed rhetoric of its own. This philosophical rhetoric is developed in a tradition that has denied its existence. The four stages are designed to expose and examine the philosophical rhetoric or imaginary that has arisen out of this peculiar situation. They can be instructive in doing so, but again need not be applied strictly. Indeed, Le Doeuff never explicitly refers to them when reading imagery, and I shall not do so either.

The first stage is that of *denegation*. It calls attention to the denial that often precedes images into a philosophical text. An image is introduced into the text, yet at the same time it is denied any (genuine) significance. Le Doeuff provides an example from *Critique of Pure Reason*, where Kant twice distances himself from the island of truth that he introduces. Le Doeuff concludes:

> Thus between the writing subject and his text there is a complex and negating relationship, which is a sign that something important and troubling is seeking utterance – something which cannot be acknowledged, yet is keenly cherished. As far as I am concerned, taking an interest

in images and enquiring into this sort of evasion are one and the same
activity. (Le Doeuff 1989: 8–9)

Denegation describes a common attitude of philosophers towards the imagery in their texts. Images are not a real part of the text, but instead they are
directed to an (irrational) Other, who does not grasp the philosophical
argument. Yet, because the 'image is not part of the enterprise . . . the good
reader, who has passed through the philosophical discipline, will know he
should pass it by' (Le Doeuff 1989: 7). Even when the use of imagery is
acknowledged, as it is especially by Le Doeuff, but also by Murdoch, this
stage can be significant. The author may recognize the limits and inconclu-
siveness of thought as well as a philosopher's dependence on other than pure
rational thought, but philosophical reading habits change only slowly.[21]

The second stage is that of *iconographic investigation*. In this stage it is asked
whether the image is a hapax, an isolated feature in the text, or whether it
occurs in other places as well. This stage again is intended to reveal the peculiar nature of the philosophical rhetoric. It is argued that it is important to
look for recurrences of any image, for these may reveal the significance of the
image encountered and suggest whether or not one has to do with a structural element in the thought of the thinker. This stage, as well as the third
stage, originates in the supposition that an image is more difficult to recognize as such, when it has become a recurrent element of the debate.[22]

The third stage is that of *erudition*. It looks for earlier usages of the image
by philosophers, attempting to locate a precise source. Le Doeuff explains
this strategy in 'Red Ink in the Margin', one of the essays in *The Philosophical
Imaginary*. In the preface she only states 'its main principle: it is a good thing
not only to bear in mind all the earlier usages of an image by philosophers
but also to locate a precise source, an image which, at the level of the signif-
ier, is close to the one being studied' (Le Doeuff 1989: 9). Borrowing an
image from a particular source, Le Doeuff argues in 'Red Ink', is to continue
'a philosopheme' in that source without argument. Le Doeuff urges her
reader to consider the image both as it appears in the source and as its trans-
formation in the present text (Le Doeuff 1989: 92ff.). Imagery, it is implied,
gains in importance when it has become part of a tradition, not just part of
the oeuvre of one thinker. It is then also more difficult to acknowledge its
presence. Le Doeuff more than once argues how this is particularly true for
the image of woman.[23]

The last phase is that of *structural analysis*. Le Doeuff calls this the essential
stage in which one looks for the 'sensitive or problematic theoretical point an
image bears on', which is often difficult to find (Le Doeuff 1989: 10). This
stage brings together the previous stages in order to detect what the role is

of the imagery whose presence is denied. Le Doeuff distinguishes here between an image's *emblematic* and its *fantasy* function. In its emblematic role the image produces a dogma.

> Images are the means by which every philosophy can engage in straight-forward dogmatization, and decree a 'that's the way it is' without fear of counter-argument, since it is understood that a good reader will by-pass such 'illustrations' − a convention which enables the image to do its work all the more effectively. (Le Doeuff 1989: 12)

On the subjective or fantasy level the image seduces its readers into accept-ing it. It does so, Le Doeuff maintains, by opposing a more general imagery, which it claims it can do without. This general imagery is replaced by parti-cular imagery, appealing only to a specific group (Le Doeuff 1989: 14ff.). One fantasy is replaced by another fantasy, even though it is presented as if all fantasy is abolished. Analysing imagery is then also emancipatory, as in the analysis the excluding nature of the philosophy becomes apparent and may be criticized. For Le Doeuff, analysing the 'particularism of a social minority and its problematic encounter with other thought and other dis-courses' will also result in 'an appreciation of the tension between what one would like to believe, what it is necessary to think and what it is possible to give logical form' (Le Doeuff 1989: 19).

The four stages thus intend to reveal rhetoric, which is designed to be dis-regarded. Imagery has had the important function of maintaining an understanding of what philosophy is or should be like, and yet it has seldom received recognition by philosophers. Le Doeuff's methodological propositions suggest that this problem is not limited to individual texts or even the work of particular authors. Rather, the stages of iconographic investigation and erudition confirm the opposite. Imagery, while being denied any relevance, often upholds established convictions to the exclusion of forms of reasoning and of social groups. In different texts Le Doeuff has shown how this is in particular true for the image of woman and the exclu-sion of women from doing philosophy.

These methodological propositions sharply diverge from an understand-ing of philosophy as distinguished from rhetoric, which at least in theory, Le Doeuff maintains, philosophers profess to hold. Of the different reasons for this divergence the most important for Le Doeuff is philosophy's attempt at self-justification. With this notion she refers to an understanding of philo-sophy in which it justifies itself and is independent of any other discipline. Philosophy is understood to rely on nothing but itself, even or in particu-lar for its foundations. However, in contrast, philosophers acknowledging and investigating the imagery used may often challenge a reader's expectations of the text, as Le Doeuff's writings have shown to do.

The Philosopher-Fool

By means of her methodological propositions Le Doeuff is the guide into the world of the philosophical imaginary, but she is an unusual guide. It has been noted that it is not easy to characterize her philosophy. Colin Gordon, in his note preceding his translation of *The Philosophical Imaginary*, asks and answers the 'unavoidable' question:

> Where . . . is Michèle Le Doeuff to be located on the maps of contemporary French philosophy and feminism? The shortest answer, and one which the author might herself favour, would be: elsewhere, or nowhere. Her writing is singularly bare of the period's usual fashionable impedimenta; it shows no systemic affiliation, no signs of a formative debt or repudiation. (Gordon 1989: vii)

Le Doeuff's philosophy is then in no obvious way described by an -ism or -ean. Or, as she puts it, quoting Moi's characterization, in an article entitled 'Vive la différence': ' "There are some feminists who are Derridians, like Sarah Kofman, and others who are not, like Michèle Le Doeuff." Long live that difference, certainly' (Le Doeuff 1991: 324 n. 9).

In his introduction to *Michèle Le Doeuff: Operative Philosophy and Imaginary Practice* Deutscher similarly remarks on the difficulty of characterizing her work (Deutscher 2000: 9). His introduction is preceded, however, by a quotation from *Hipparchia's Choice*, which reveals a possible reason for these difficulties. At the beginning of *Hipparchia's Choice* Le Doeuff describes how her inspiration to become a philosopher was preceded by a childhood desire to be a Shakespearean fool. After initial disappointment that life was not written by Shakespeare, that there were no fools around and that Shakespeare's fools were all men, she found the possibility to live by this aspiration in philosophy:

> Looking back it seems to me that what had seduced me in the Shakespearian characters was already philosophy. With their sarcastic and corrosive utterances, their unseasonable taste for truth without pomposity, their corruption of words and their art of impertinence which forces authority, sometimes royal authority, to enter into their irony, my fools were the distant heirs of Socrates, of Diogenes the Cynic, of Epictetus and many others. One day Aristippus of Cyrene was asked what benefits he had

gained from philosophy. And he, whom they called 'the royal dog', replied: 'that of being able to speak freely to everyone.' Shakespearian characters are certainly closer to the Greek philosophers than Auguste Comte ever was. (Le Doeuff 1991: 9–10)[24]

Thus in the first pages of *Hipparchia's Choice* Le Doeuff proclaims to be a philosopher and a fool. As if to demonstrate this particular disposition she adds the rather shrewd remark on Comte and Socrates which concludes the paragraph. Such remarks, she seems to suggest, one should expect from an author of 'sarcastic and corrosive utterances', from 'a corrupter of words', from someone with 'an unseasonable taste for truth without pomposity' and her 'art of impertinence which forces authority, sometimes royal authority, to enter into [her] irony'.

Even though Le Doeuff emphasizes that philosopher-fools are not exceptional in the history of philosophy, her defensive remark on Comte illustrates that this image is not undisputed either. To speak of the wisdom of fools, or desired by fools, is a deliberate twist on the prevalent image, where fools are regarded as the opposite of wise, and philosophers (as their name gives away) desire wisdom. Philosophers don't fool around. Even the fools that have been introduced into philosophical work to show its strength are not silly or simple-minded. Rather they are intelligent but reluctant to appreciate an argument or its conclusion.[25] To convince such fools may indicate reason's strength, as even those who are not sympathetic to what is argued have to yield to the conclusion. A famous example of such a fool is of course found in Anselm's *Proslogion*.[26]

The fool presents an ambiguous image. Hence, it should not be surprising that the writing of one who calls herself a fool is not easily characterized. Closer analysis of the image of the fool is needed. Such an analysis is also expedient because this image appears in the work of an author who claims that her first interest is always in imagery.[27] Moreover, the image appears at a pivotal stage in *Hipparchia's Choice*. It is introduced at a point where self-validation seems unavoidable. Is it worth writing on women and philosophy as Le Doeuff proposes to do? Yet self-validation is what Le Doeuff most criticizes philosophy for. Her recurrent argument is that philosophy can only be self-validating at the expense of exclusion. It needs to exclude what is other: images, primitives, women (see, for example, Le Doeuff 1989: 6–7, and Le Doeuff 1991: 26). Le Doeuff then tries to avoid self-validation and its unfortunate consequences, but is unable to do so without stating *what she herself values in philosophy*. At this point, where a premature collapse in contradiction is looming, Le Doeuff introduces the fool. The fool is in a way Le Doeuff's founding myth.

Regarding these reasons for examining the image of the fool, it is remarkable that in most commentaries it is not even mentioned. Deutscher cites part of Le Doeuff's text introducing this image, but he does not entertain the image in his introduction. Sanders includes the fool in an article on the use of the concepts 'philosophy' and 'rationality' in feminist writing. She argues that for Le Doeuff the fool is the connection between the past and the future of philosophy: 'The perspective of the fool was always an important part of philosophy ... and it will represent the best of the philosophy of the future' (Sanders 1993: 426). Here the image of the fool depicts the acceptance of the limitations of philosophy in its dependence on other forms of writing, as well as a critical stance towards any theory. Sanders does not pursue this image in the main argument of her article (Sanders 1993: 425–426).

The short autobiographical piece on the philosopher-fool starts with a striking juxtaposition of desire and seduction on the one hand and conquest on the other: 'It is impossible to see how such a desire [i.e. to do philosophy] can be rationalized or deduced from an essence of philosophy of such great value that one would be conquered on first perceiving it and would decide to devote all one's energy to it' (Le Doeuff 1991: 9). The expressed desire to do philosophy cannot be transformed into a defeating philosophical argument (cf. Le Doeuff 2003: 14). Instead, Le Doeuff presents the autobiographical story of herself as a child seduced into the world of Shakespeare, wanting to become Feste, or the fool in *King Lear*.

Le Doeuff's affair with philosophy is then not a story of conquest but of seduction. As a child she felt a passion for Shakespeare, yet when growing up she realized that he would not give her the role she desired most in his world. It was one of the few parts he would not let women play: 'Shakespeare played on sexual identity to the maximum, but he could not go so far as to imagine a certain form of comic utterance spoken by a female character.'[28] Moreover, his world did not exist. Life, if written at all, was written by someone else. Fortunately, Le Doeuff did not have to forfeit her first love, for in philosophy she found 'approximate fulfilment' (Mortley 1991: 83) of her desires in an actually existing world. As a student at a French *lycée* she was even obliged to take the part.

Philosophers rarely admit to being seduced. In her article on Le Doeuff and the myths of the Sirens, Bassett observes that '[t]he voice of the Sirens is perilous if you are open to its seduction, but if you are a philosopher, you are protected by rigor and thus are able to be seduced without harm' (Bassett 2000: 106; cf. Le Doeuff 1989: 129–137). Cunning as Odysseus, philosophers have let themselves be safely tied to the mast. In turn, they may seduce mere mortals, who are not in danger either, because the philosopher's rigour protects all from shipwreck.

By admitting to being seduced, therefore, does Le Doeuff reveal she is lacking philosophical rigour? Or, by acting the seduced and not the conquering part, does she confirm the image of woman as other than philosopher? Le Doeuff often makes jokes about stereotypes of women, and thus about herself, but there is always a worry that such jokes are taken seriously. If women and philosophy still do not go together naturally, as Le Doeuff maintains in *Hipparchia's Choice*, it may not be expedient to align with philosophy's fools, who cannot or do not want to understand the philosopher's argument and will only yield at the very end. Playing the fool is fun, but what if having fun is not wise, not even close to *desiring* wisdom? How can women be taken seriously as philosophers? As women? As both?

Le Doeuff, however, is seduced into a world where 'sexual identity is played on to the maximum'. This is a world in which women play male roles.[29] Viola, Portia and Rosalind all pretend to be men. To complicate matters, in the original casts men enacted the role of these women who were in turn disguised as men. Lear's fool is so close to Cordelia that when Lear exclaims that his 'poor fool is hanged' (*King Lear*, V.iii.306) one can think of either. In fact, one actor may play on both parts, for they are never on stage together. Shakespeare thus plays sexual identity to the maximum, even though the sexually most ambiguous role of all, that of the fool, is given to men only.

Introducing the Shakespearean fool into philosophy implies that the problem of women and philosophy is not just or perhaps not even a problem of women playing men's parts.[30] The question of how women can be philosophers and women, where philosophy has notoriously seen 'woman' as that which it is not, is not dissolved by recasting the parts (Le Doeuff 1987: 42, 51ff.). By putting forward the image of the fool Le Doeuff adds an extra dimension to this problem. The (philosopher-)king is not recast as the (philosopher-)queen, but as the sexually more ambiguous (philosopher-)fool. Recasting here does not simply mean replacing, for the fool is known to subvert hierarchical order.

The fool is also a marginal figure. He is only indirectly involved in the major developments of the play.[31] Tradition has occasionally brushed him aside.[32] Nevertheless, his comments are persistent and also uncompromising. As Sanders maintains, the fool has 'no need to justify himself by over-inflated and unfounded arguments because his position is one which, unlike the King's, does not need to convince others because he is not demanding anything of them' (Sanders 1993: 426). This position grants the fool a form of authority, namely that of one who, as Le Doeuff states, can have an 'unseasonable taste for truth without pomposity'.

Thus by calling herself a fool Le Doeuff affirms (or reaffirms) her marginal position but also claims some form of authority. Authority is confirmed in other ways as well. By retracing the seduction back to childhood, it is implied that philosophy is what Le Doeuff has been doing all her life and to what she has been attracted before she was affected by society's demands and expectations. Le Doeuff is, in short, a natural philosopher. Moreover, by calling herself a fool Le Doeuff also places herself in line, not with Comte, but with illustrious philosophers nevertheless, beginning with Socrates.

Le Doeuff as a philosopher-fool is then part of an old tradition in the history of philosophy. The word tradition perhaps suggests too much cohesion. This is a 'tradition' of individuals who have singly challenged what is generally believed to be true, or beyond discussion. They may be characterized as preferring the image of fool to that of wise, or consider the fool the wiser. Even though it would be odd to speak of an -ism or -ean here, it is neither correct to consider such thinkers as entirely isolated or unique. Avoiding again a strict division between rebellious and dutiful daughters these thinkers are perhaps best characterized as valuing their independence from father, mother, or tradition.[33]

What is the relation of these fools to their Kings? It seems to me that Le Doeuff has omitted this aspect of the image. This observation adds a new dimension to Le Doeuff's methodological propositions. For Le Doeuff discusses the desired functions of an image (emblematic and fantasy), but does not mention the possibility of undesired ones. She does not mention the King against whom the fool directs his banter. Sanders argues that Le Doeuff does not 'fail to recognise that the fool's freedom is contained within the limits of the King's pleasure: when that pleasure is pushed too far the fool can always be beheaded' (Sanders 1993: 426). Le Doeuff dismisses this possibility all too easily when she remarks to Mortley on the possibility of being looked down upon that 'since a woman is doomed to scant respect anyway, it does not matter. If you have nothing to lose, you can afford to be daring' (Mortley 1991: 85). Or is she joking again?

Conclusion

The introduction of the philosophical imaginary into reading philosophy and Murdoch's philosophy affects philosophical reading habits, and philosophy's perceived practice. This chapter articulated what may seem sweeping statements about philosophy: that it is not as (gender-)neutral as it claims to be, that it excludes what is other, that it considers itself independent from other disciplines, that it defines itself in opposition to rhetoric, that it does not acknowledge its own imagery.

At no point did I want to suggest that either the history of philosophy, or its present practice, knows no exceptions to these statements. And yet, I would argue, these exceptions do not render the statements false. The presuppositions about philosophy, found in remarks by Midgley, Warnock, Nussbaum, Magee and Murdoch, I deem typical not just for these individuals. They are commonly held. Why does Magee characterize Murdoch's philosophical writing as 'transparent ... saying only one thing at a time', when her writing is so obviously full of ambiguous imagery? Why does Murdoch agree?

It is necessary to become aware of one's own philosophical reading habits when studying Murdoch's philosophical work. Too often have I heard the complaint that Murdoch does not provide any argument, though it is rarely noted that she was the first to question the nature of her arguments. Philosophy is not the neutral discipline it claims to be. Like other disciplines it has been formed by a privileged group of people. Their preferences have decided the discipline. Yet, now that philosophy is being practised by a more diverse group of people, the limitations of these preferences and their supposed neutrality need to be questioned. Philosophy needs to recognize its own rhetoric.

To argue for philosophy's rhetoric will change the discipline considerably, as shown by Le Doeuff. Le Doeuff is a guide into the world of the philosophical imaginary, but an unusual one. She provides methodological instruction, but also a notion of philosophy that deliberately undermines the methodology. Crucial concepts are left without much definition. She does not impose what an image is, what philosophy is, or who is a philosopher. These are questions she does not want philosophy to decide in advance. Le Doeuff describes herself as fond of sarcastic and corrosive utterances and of truth without pomposity, which leaves the reader to wonder which is what. Her philosopher-fool is not one who wants to take us by the hand.[34] On the contrary, with a philosopher-fool one should be constantly alert, both to the banter and to the truth. The distinction between teacher and student is only one of the many that the fool subverts. With a fool one is forced to think for oneself. The work of Le Doeuff challenges important and strongly held assumptions from the history of philosophy. Some are so established that they are hardly recognized as such. Her work encourages recognition and even defiance of reading habits suggested by tradition or by actual texts. It calls attention to the metaphors, imagery and stories in a philosophical text, which philosophical reading habit has often decreed to ignore.

Her 'methodological propositions', as well as the more general observations on the presence of imagery in philosophy, have inspired the subsequent reading of Murdoch. This inspiration is not always marked. My reading pursues the importance Murdoch attributes to metaphors, even beyond the possibilities Murdoch foresees or would perhaps accept. This is true, for example, when reading the image of M and D in the subsequent chapter.

Literature, Character and Philosophy

Introduction

The first kind of imagery to consider in Murdoch's philosophical work consists of the various references to literature, in general as well as specific works. These references can be considered as imagery when they work in a way described by Le Doeuff: they assert a certain value that cannot be or has not been asserted in any other way. The depiction of character in what Murdoch boldly calls 'the nineteenth century novel' does exactly that. It emphasizes the importance for moral philosophy of the inner life – of musing and daydream – in relation to a robust outside reality, when Murdoch is not yet able to find philosophical arguments.

Neither of the philosophies prominent in Murdoch's early writing – existentialism and analytical philosophy – has much interest in the inner life, or develops an understanding of a significantly different reality.[1] And yet, both philosophies were of great importance for Murdoch's thought – especially up to the publication of *The Sovereignty of Good* (1970). Their importance is acknowledged by all commentators. Some emphasize analytical philosophy, others existentialism. This chapter thus introduces two streams of thought that each in its own way helped form Murdoch's own thought. 'Helped form', however, should not be understood in a merely constructive way. Even though Murdoch has acknowledged the merits of each, she has come to posit her own thought more and more in opposition to these two. When in 'The Sublime and the Beautiful Revisited' (1959) Murdoch presents the images of Ordinary Language Man and Totalitarian Man she expresses criticism more than appreciation. Ordinary Language Man is here the man of contemporary British philosophy, Totalitarian Man of (Sartrean) existentialism.

In this chapter I approach Murdoch's texts from the following perspective. In the first, introductory chapter I reflected on the relationship between literature and philosophy in Murdoch's work. I argued that whereas the influence of the philosophy on the literature has received ample consideration, this is not true for the influence of literature on philosophy. In the present chapter I pursue this insight, yet considering not so much Murdoch's novels as her understanding of literature. Literature, and in particular the nineteenth-century novel, provides for her values that she does not find in contemporary philosophy.

In the first part of this chapter I discuss how these values (the importance of inner life and reality outside the self) are taken from her understanding of character, and how they have usually been discussed. In the second part I discuss how Murdoch looks for these values when considering existentialism. From the various reasons she may have had for being attracted to existentialism I focus on its representation of consciousness. I argue that Murdoch is in the end disappointed by existentialism, for its understanding of inner life does not endorse evaluation by an independent reality. Her later criticism of existentialism concerns most of all the similarities to linguistic analysis, most importantly its emphasis on will. Existentialism has been an important, but also passing, concern for Murdoch's thought. In the third part of this chapter I focus on the example of M and D in 'The Idea of Perfection'.

The Ills of Philosophy and Literature

This book argues for the importance of Murdoch's understanding of literature and especially the literary trope of character for her philosophical thought. In doing so, it diverges from most other discussions of this notion. Murdoch's observations on the nineteenth-century novel and its notion of character have not been considered by philosophers as much as by literary theorists. Especially in the early criticism, they have been judged in relation to her own novels. In contrast, I shall argue that Murdoch intended her remarks to have a much wider scope, or perhaps a rather different scope.

A wider scope is also suggested by Conradi, entitling the sixth part of *Existentialists and Mystics* 'Can Literature Help Cure the Ills of Philosophy?'. This heading is inspired by the following quotation from 'Against Dryness' (1961): 'Literature, in curing its own ills, can give us a new vocabulary of experience and a truer picture of freedom' (Murdoch 1997: 259; cf. 295). The full quotation then suggests that, contrary to what Conradi's title implies, the ills are not only philosophical but also literary.[2] One would then be mistaken to think of philosophy as the problem and literature as the answer. Rather, Murdoch considers both contemporary philosophy and contemporary literature to be suffering from the same ill: 'far too shallow and flimsy an idea of human personality' (Murdoch 1997: 287; cf. Antonaccio 2000: 107–111).

This contraction of all analytical, or even all contemporary, philosophy to a unified theory or even personage is quite common in Murdoch's work.[3] In 'The Sublime and the Beautiful Revisited' she introduces Ordinary Language Man as the man of 'linguistic empiricism' and Totalitarian Man as the man of 'Sartrean existentialism' (Murdoch 1997: 267–270). In 'Vision and Choice' she speaks of 'the "current view"', apologizing to those who do not hold it (Murdoch 1997: 77). In 'Metaphysics and Ethics' she explains her use of the term 'modern philosophers and modern philosophy' as 'that present-day version of our traditional empiricism which is known as linguistic analysis' (Murdoch 1997: 59).

Murdoch perceives the contemporary (analytical) philosophers around her as a fairly harmonized assembly, with Ryle, Hare and Hampshire as its most significant members. Although she touches on the differences between her contemporaries, such comparisons do not appear frequently and do not have much significance, for even in these comparisons Murdoch stresses the features these philosophers share (see for example Murdoch 1997: 69). She considers her main criticism so fundamental that it bypasses minor points of contrast and affects the different philosophers equally. In later work Murdoch even combines her criticism of analytical philosophy and existentialism in one image, as in the rather frightening imagery in 'On "God" and "Good"', where existentialism is set to be 'capable of . . . getting into the minds' of Oxford philosophers, who may not have looked for it and may not even be aware of it (Murdoch 1997: 337–338).

In the same spirit Murdoch argues in 'Against Dryness' that both analytical and existentialist philosophy display a similar poor picture of human beings. She focuses on the image in analytical philosophy, while arguing that any difference with existentialist philosophy is not essential. 'Against Dryness' presents in a few lines what is wrong with the understanding of human beings in moral philosophy. Human beings are reduced to 'free rational wills', without any sense of a transcending reality or value.[4] These human beings will never meet any real others, or encounter any overpowering reality.[5] Instead, they oversee their surroundings and express their beliefs in acts and choices: 'We picture man as a brave naked will surrounded by an easily comprehended empirical world' (Murdoch 1997: 290). These are the ills affecting literature and philosophy. And without curing these ills, Murdoch implies, 'we' cannot 'recover from two wars and the experience of Hitler' (Murdoch 1997: 287). In other words, we cannot become morally better.

The close connection between literature and philosophy is not exceptional, but found throughout Murdoch's work. She naturally thinks in literary imagery and easily switches between philosophy and fiction.

In 'Thinking and Language', for example, one of the earliest essays, Murdoch interjects the musing of Gwendolen from George Eliot's *Daniel Deronda*, in order to argue that inner monologues are relevant in themselves, not only with regard to subsequent overt actions and choices. The scene from *Daniel Deronda* is presented to dispute the assumed insignificance of mental events in philosophy: it matters very much to Gwendolen whether she intended the death of her husband, when she hesitated to throw the life-belt to him. Similarly, 'we' consider 'our' internal monologues important, and want to make sense of them. 'We', who recognize what Gwendolen endures, are contrasted to an 'external observer'. Murdoch here equates thinking about fictional characters and about 'us' (Murdoch 1997: 36).

Literature appears to be part of the opposition between ordinary and philosophical, which runs through the essay. Murdoch, while engaging in philosophical arguments, positions herself in opposition to philosophy. So, she writes at the beginning of the essay: 'I set aside all philosophical theories, old and new', or 'I shall assume, as we all do when we are not philosophising . . .' (Murdoch 1997: 33). In her philosophical writings she engages literary examples as representing the ordinary or recognizable, and places these in opposition to the philosophical. Literature embodies what Murdoch calls ordinary.

However, *this* literature is not the same as the literature suffering from ills, mentioned above. The exemplary literature is the literature of the past, more specifically what Murdoch refers to as the nineteenth-century novel. This notion includes works of a diverse range of authors: Austen, Scott, George Eliot, Henry James and above all Tolstoy. These authors she compares favourably to works in another (disparate) group: the twentieth-century novel. She expresses this distinction most succinctly in 'Existentialists and Mystics'. Nineteenth-century novels differ most obviously from twentieth-century novels in being better. But this is not the only difference. Nineteenth-century novels also differ from twentieth-century ones in still being able to take society more or less for granted. Society is real, and so is the human mind (Murdoch 1997: 221). In 'Against Dryness' Murdoch similarly argues that the nineteenth-century novel 'was concerned with real various individuals struggling in society' (Murdoch 1997: 291).

This substantial nature of the nineteenth-century characters Murdoch unmistakably prefers to those she encounters in the twentieth-century novel. The twentieth-century novel she considers no longer to present those real individuals. In 'Against Dryness' Murdoch suggests that the twentieth-century novel is either 'crystalline or journalistic'.[6] A crystalline novel is 'a small quasi-allegorical object portraying the human condition and not containing "characters" in the nineteenth-century sense'. A journalistic novel, in contrast, is 'a large shapeless quasi-documentary object, the degenerate descendant of the nineteenth-century novel, telling, with pale conventional characters, some straightforward story enlivened with empirical facts' (Murdoch 1997: 291). Neither crystalline nor journalistic novels then contain real characters. They are either not present, or only shadows of characters in the nineteenth-century novel. Twentieth-century novelists fail at the creation of character, something which Murdoch considers central to any writer's work (Murdoch 1997: 253).

That nineteenth-century novels are obviously better, in Murdoch's serious jest, or that they are most concerned with a portrayal of character, which challenges the demands of an overarching form, can be and has been disputed. Only a few years after the first publication of 'Against Dryness', Hillis Miller, in his *The Form of Victorian Fiction* (1968), considered Victorian novels as structures in which the characters fit into the whole: 'Every element draws its meaning from the others, so that the novel must be described as a self-generating and self-sustaining system' (Hillis Miller 1968: 30). Bergonzi, in his *The Situation of the Novel* (1979), points out that the enduring faith in character expressed by Murdoch in the quotation above is not universal, but predominantly British: 'On the Continent it seems to be assumed that the realistic novel of character has had its day; while American critics are agreed that it has never properly flourished in the United States.' In Britain, in contrast, 'it is widely held that such novels can and should go on being written' (Bergonzi 1979: 42). In this context Bergonzi discusses the work of Bayley and Murdoch.

However, most texts dealing with Murdoch's novels rarely challenge her understanding of the nineteenth-century novel. Instead, her comments on the nineteenth- and twentieth-century novel have been examined almost exclusively in relation to her own novels. Such an examination has been encouraged by the explicit recommendation that Murdoch provides. At the end of 'Against Dryness', for instance, she argues that literature needs to change, so as to bring about a return to picturing 'in a non-metaphysical, non-totalitarian and non-religious sense, the transcendence of reality' (Murdoch 1997: 293). In doing so, literature will cure both its own ills and those of philosophy, for 'it has taken over some of the tasks performed by philosophy' (Murdoch 1997: 294).

The change needed is, Murdoch suggests, a return to 'the now so unfashionable naturalistic idea of character'. Murdoch's explanation here veers significantly between appealing to reality and to literary construction. Thus she pleads for the return of character, only to explain that '[r]eal people are destructive of myth'. Real people stop fantasy and encourage a return of imagination – as the Russian novels show so well. Similarly, she calls literature 'a battle between people and images', explaining that a 'much stronger and more complex *conception* of the former' is needed (Murdoch 1997: 294–295, emphasis added). Murdoch thus engages her understanding of character in a battle against the form, or myth, of the crystalline novel. Character as a 'destructive power' defies the self-contained or whole. Thinking of the Russians one may recognize how real people and contingency destroy fantasy and make way for imagination.

It seems appropriate to relate these recommendations to Murdoch's novels, as it is unlikely that they do not in one way or another relate to the difficulties Murdoch experienced herself when writing novels. So, her plea in this essay for 'the now so unfashionable naturalistic idea of character' has been pivotal for early critics in particular, in the appraisal of her novels. Yet the verdict has been far from uniform. Some critics consider Murdoch's novels to come up to her own theoretical standards whereas others find them decidedly failing. When applying these ideas to her own novels literary critics have been outspoken, yet they have also assumed the straightforwardness of their assessment. For example, Bergonzi writes after the quotation on the importance of character given above that 'it will be *evident* to the readers of Miss Murdoch's innumerable novels that she has conspicuously failed to put her ideas into practice, at least since *The Bell* came out in 1958' (Bergonzi 1979: 47, emphasis added). Indeed, he argues that the characters may be complex, but they cannot interact as real people. Instead, 'they can relate to each other only by some form of arbitrary sexual encounter, or an act of violence, or by involvement in the complicated or dangerous physical activity that Miss Murdoch describes rather well' (Bergonzi 1979: 48). For Bergonzi, even though the characters in Murdoch's novels may be rather complex, form plays the main part. However, where for Bergonzi Murdoch evidently fails, Conradi is adamant as well as brief in his defence of her: 'As to her supposed relative poverty at depicting character, however, her work everywhere gainsays this judgement.'[7]

Both assertive assessments further explain the notion of character, though questions remain. The opposition between form and individual may suffice in pointing to lack of character, but it is less efficient in showing the presence of character. Even the – for Murdoch – obvious examples from the nineteenth century can be contested. What then is character? When is a character sufficiently sturdy to resist the patterns of the novel? As these are the issues Murdoch struggles with as a novelist, a ready answer cannot be expected. The examples of the past do not necessarily reveal the solution for the present or the future. Yet, in presenting the problem of 'far too shallow and flimsy an idea of human personality' by means of the notion of character, Murdoch makes clear that the problem is not one of individuals, but of relationship. Are the characters subject to the author's structure, or can he or she allow them independence? 'To understand other people is a task which does not come to an end' (Murdoch 1997: 283).

Murdoch also suggests that at least part of the answer comes in terms of use of language, when lamenting: 'Most modern English novels indeed are not *written*. One feels they could slip into some other medium without much loss' (Murdoch 1997: 292, emphasis in original). A brief consideration of her novels may elucidate how Murdoch struggles here, and not always successfully. In his review of *The Red and the Green* Ricks cites Murdoch's (theoretical) appreciation of 'history, real beings and real change, whatever is contingent, messy, boundless, infinitely particular and endlessly still to be explained', yet finds that her routine use of words like ' "[m]ystery" and its derivatives, "vague", "sinister", "strange", "obscure", "curious", "somehow", "weird", "eerie", "alarming", "appalling" ' as well as ' "a sort of", "a kind of" ' abandons any sense of mystery. He concludes: 'The adjective duress and the formulaic repetitiveness of her style undo any independent life in the characters.' Like Byatt, Ricks quotes Murdoch's words when assessing that she, like Sartre, is unable to teach that 'the human person is precious and unique; but we seem unable to set it forth except in terms of ideology and abstraction' (Ricks 1965: 605; cf. Byatt 1994: 209 and Murdoch 1999: 148).

Murdoch's practice as a novelist and her appreciation of literature thus underlie her systematic thinking. The nineteenth-century novel provides an ideal, to which she as a contemporary novelist seems unable to aspire, but which allows her to criticize contemporary philosophy. Nicol, in a recent article, similarly argues that 'certain of her key philosophical concerns might usefully be regarded as fundamentally *literary* problems'. More specifically, quoting 'Art is the Imitation of Nature', he suggests that storytelling is 'Murdoch's chief preoccupation throughout her writing career, which dominated both her moral philosophy and her fiction'. Again, the issue is not to impose too much structure when telling the story (Nicol 2006: 100, 101, emphasis in original).

Murdoch's recommendations for the creation of character may thus have arisen from her practice as a novelist, yet Murdoch is not just writing as a novelist, but rather considering both philosophy and literature. So, at the beginning of 'The Sublime and the Beautiful Revisited' she claims to 'approach the problem as a novelist concerned with the creation of character'.[8] Yet contrary to one's expectations, this remark is followed by a short history of the notion of the individual in philosophy, starting with Kant. Conversely, in the second part of the essay, when turning to literature Murdoch claims that she is not a critic, but that she is 'doing what philosophers do' (Murdoch 1997: 270). This alternation between Murdoch the novelist and Murdoch the philosopher suggests that Murdoch does not limit herself here to one discipline (cf. Murdoch 1997: 289).

Conradi's question, then, 'Can Literature Help Cure the Ills of Philosophy?', encourages to consider Murdoch's concern with character in a larger perspective. As a novelist concerned with the creation of character Murdoch turns to philosophy. As a philosopher concerned with the individual she turns to novels. So, Murdoch is not only talking about her own novels, but more generally about contemporary literature and philosophy. Her attempts to reintroduce a less flimsy notion of the self not only concern her novels but also her philosophical writing. As the contemporary analytical philosophy was hardly interested in the self, Murdoch turned to existentialism as a philosophy that in its interest in literature also promised to be a philosophy interested in inner life.

The Merits of Existentialism

It has been argued that Murdoch's turn to existentialism was motivated by 'her deep dissatisfaction with Anglo-Saxon philosophy'. The attraction of existentialism lies in its interest in consciousness and in moral value. She did not find this interest in the contemporary philosophy she encountered in Oxford and Cambridge.[9]

Sartre's philosophy was very popular after the war. In the 1987 introduction to *Sartre: Romantic Rationalist* Murdoch vividly recalls the atmosphere of excitement it created. Sartre, she writes, was one of the very few philosophers whose popularity has been with large masses of young people all over Europe, even more than with professional philosophers:

> It had long been known that God was dead and that man was self-created. Sartre produced a fresh and apt picture of this self-chosen being. . . . The war was over, Europe was in ruins, we had emerged from a long captivity, all was to be remade. Sartre's philosophy was an inspiration to many who felt that they must, and *could*, make out of all that misery and chaos a better world, for it had now been revealed that anything was possible. Existentialism was the new religion, the new salvation. This was the atmosphere in Brussels in 1945 where I first read *L'Être et le Néant* and where I briefly (and on this occasion only) met Sartre. His presence in the city was like that of a pop star. Chico Marx, who was there at about the same time, was less rapturously received. (Murdoch 1999: 9–10)

Murdoch's appreciation for existentialism is not only with the 'fresh and apt picture of a self-chosen being', but also with the abundant enthusiasm with which this image was perceived as 'the new religion, the new salvation'. When in later writing she is mainly critical of existentialism, she still praises its attempt and desire 'to be a philosophy one could live by. Kierkegaard described the Hegelian system as a grand palace set up by someone who then lived in a hovel or at best in the porter's lodge. A moral philosophy should be inhabited' (Murdoch 1997: 337). Existentialism Murdoch deemed habitable, yet if she ever moved in, she did not stay long.[10] In her later work, the term becomes synonymous for her criticism of all contemporary philosophy, whether analytical or continental.

Murdoch must also have been drawn towards Sartre's oeuvre, because it too joins works of literature with works of philosophy. Thus, David Gordon suggests that '[t]he subject of *Sartre: Romantic Rationalist* must have recommended itself readily to someone of her generation who was well trained in philosophy and about to publish a novel' (Gordon 1995: 17). Similarly, Spear writes that '[i]t is perhaps very much a pointer to her underlying interests at the time that the book [*Sartre: Romantic Rationalist*], although essentially a philosophical study, is based on a consideration of Sartre's novels which, [Murdoch] suggests, "provide more comprehensive material for a study of his thought"'.[11] Yet, Murdoch observes that Sartre's, De Beauvoir's and Camus' concern for literature is more than fortuitous. 'These writers would claim that they are philosophers in the main tradition of European philosophy – and that their use of literary means is symptomatic of the turn that philosophy as a whole is now taking', she argues in a broadcast for the BBC in 1950 (Murdoch 1997: 101). Murdoch sounds almost prophetic here. Philosophy as a whole is taking a literary turn. Even if it is not true for all of philosophy, it will be for hers. There is also a remarkable difference between this broadcast and 'Against Dryness', eleven years later. In 1950 Murdoch is still exploring existentialism's possibilities. Ten years later her tone is much more critical. In 1950 she predicts that philosophy will take a literary turn. In 1961, she will argue that literature will assume some of philosophy's tasks.

In the broadcast Murdoch argues that Sartre's novels have 'a strictly didactic purpose'. They make their readers aware that humans are both free and lonely, and that the only way to face the world sincerely is as these free, lonely individuals (Murdoch 1997: 103–104). Existentialism has clearly no desire to remain neutral. In the modern world without God it prescribes certain understanding and meaning. Human beings are free and lonely. Human consciousness is understood in relation to things. Consciousness is, in Sartre's well-known phrase, '*être-pour-soi*', being-for-itself, and things are '*être-en-soi*', being-in-itself. The '*en-soi*' Sartre explains as being that is what it is (Sartre 2003: 18ff). It is complete identity. Consciousness, in contrast, Murdoch argues, 'is not a substance and it has no meaning, although it is the source of all meaning. Its fundamental character is nothingness, that is, its freedom' (Murdoch 1997: 104).[12] Human beings are not just free, they are *condemned* to freedom. They have the obligation to be free. The realization of this obligation creates dread. Human consciousness has to determine itself. It has to decide what to believe, what to do, what to avoid, and cannot rely on anything else in doing so. It has to be wary of all efforts to make it into a thing, or an '*en-soi*'. Consciousness 'has to contend, not only with the world of things, but with other selves who are only too ready to make it an object in their universe and to give it their alien significance' (Murdoch 1997: 104). In Sartre's existentialism people are fundamentally alone in an inimical world.

It is this condition that Sartre's novels describe. Murdoch concludes that these novels are a new kind of novel 'in the sense that the writer's attention is focused on this unusual point, this point at which our beliefs, our world pictures, our politics, religions, loves and hates are seen to be discontinuous with the selves that may or may not go on affirming them' (Murdoch 1997: 107). This is a remarkable observation with the hindsight of her later writing. The existentialist novel queries the relation between society and self, which makes, for Murdoch, the nineteenth-century novel so good. In this broadcast, Murdoch introduces a new form of writing, which she considers as providing exciting possibilities for describing what it is like to live and give meaning to one's life in a world without God. In later writing this lonely man, whom she recognizes in most novels, embodies a much criticized understanding of human being. In 1950 she is primarily fascinated by the discontinuity of world and self. Ten years later she considers it part of a fundamental problem.

The shift from enthusiasm to more sober judgement is explained by *Sartre: Romantic Rationalist*, particularly by the discussion of *La Nausée* and its main character Antoine Roquentin. When pressed by Magee to consider a possible role for philosophy in literature this first novel of Sartre's is 'one good philosophical novel' she can think of, for it 'does manage to express some interesting ideas about contingency and consciousness, and to remain a work of art which does not have to be read in the light of theories which the author has expressed elsewhere'.[13] Murdoch's strongest as well as lasting fascination rests, I would argue, not so much with existentialism's general picture as with Antoine Roquentin. Her interest in Roquentin lasts from her early writings to the last, *Metaphysics as a Guide to Morals*.

Sartre: Romantic Rationalist testifies to Murdoch's fascination with *La Nausée*. The novel is discussed in the first chapter, as an unorthodox introduction to Sartre's work. *Sartre: Romantic Rationalist* is not organized

according to chronology. In fact, the work does not have much resemblance
to the more common appearance of a work on one thinker. It does not start
with a description of his life, or an attempt at an overview of his work. It is
instead ordered in a rather idiosyncratic way. *La Nausée* poses a problem, for
which Murdoch in consequent chapters looks for a solution. It is via the
image of its main character and narrator, Antoine Roquentin, presented
by *La Nausée*, that one may understand the extraordinary construction of
Sartre: Romantic Rationalist.

Roquentin is condemned to ethical and logical loneliness (Murdoch
1997: 106–107). He is a man almost without relation or conversation. Yet,
his loneliness goes far beyond that of any form of ordinary solitude. He feels
not only isolated from, but also disgusted by the mere existence of things and
people. Murdoch concisely relates his experience of horror on different
occasions. Standing on the seashore about to throw a pebble into the
water, he is suddenly overcome with 'a curious sickly horror'. Sitting in a
café, '[l]ooking at a glass of beer, at the braces of the café *patron*, he is filled
with a "sweetish sort of disgust" ' (*une espèce d'écoeurement douceâtre*) (Murdoch
1999: 39). He visits a museum full of pictures of the bourgeoisie in Bouville.
He recognizes how they claim that their lives had meaning by referring to
the institutions of state and family they belonged to and Roquentin turns
away, disgusted (Murdoch 1999: 40).

It is not just things that provoke this experience. Murdoch notes that
'what marks him out as an existentialist doubter is the fact that he himself
is in the picture: what most distresses him is that his own individual being is
invaded by the senseless flux; what most interests him is his aspiration to *be* in
a different way' (Murdoch 1999: 43, emphasis in original). The experience
of nausea is first encountered when he 'looks at his own face in the mirror,
and suddenly it seems to him inhuman, fishlike' (Murdoch 1999: 39).
Roquentin realizes that there is no inevitability in a lived life, that there
are no adventures: 'One can live or tell: not both at once.' What is the
'I' that exists presently? It is 'merely the ever-lengthening *stuff* of gluey
sensations and vague fragmentary thoughts' (Murdoch 1999: 40; emphasis
in original).

The climax and also the most metaphysical part of the story Murdoch
considers to be Roquentin's realization that word and thing are not related
at all. The word 'seagull' makes it possible to think in classes and kinds,
but he never related the word to this individual thing he now encounters
in the park.

Then comes the final and fullest revelation. 'I understood that there was
no middle way between non-existence and this swooning abundance.

What exists at all must exist to this point: the point of mouldering, of bul-
ging, of obscenity. In another world, circles and melodies retain their
pure and rigid contours. But existence is a degeneration.' (Murdoch
1999: 41)

Imprisoned between this existence and the purity he is looking for, Roquentin finds his salvation through art, through a book he will write, which will
enable him to 'attain to a conception of his own life as having the purity, the
clarity and the necessity which the work of art created by him will possess'
(Murdoch 1999: 46).

Murdoch is not much convinced by this solution and neither, she assumes,
is Sartre (Murdoch 1999: 46–47 and 50 respectively). She decides that
La Nausée's 'interest lies in the powerful image which dominates it, and
in the description which constitutes the argument' (Murdoch 1999: 47).
La Nausée is 'a philosophical myth' that 'shows to us in a memorable way
the master-image of Sartre's thinking' (Murdoch 1999: 42, 49). It is said to
describe alternately 'all of us', the philosopher and Sartre. At one point
Murdoch allows for 'Roquentin's sensations [to be] not in themselves so
rare and peculiar' (Murdoch 1999: 43), but fairly recognizable. At another
time, she denies that Roquentin is an ordinary man. He regards the world
with the reflexive consciousness of a philosopher. In an illuminating comparison to K. in Kafka's *The Castle*, Murdoch points out how despite the
absurdity of his surroundings K. keeps faith in ordinary communication
and signs, whereas Sartre's hero quickly abandons such hopes when he realizes the absurdity of the world. Murdoch concludes: 'The hero of *La Nausée*
is reflective and analytical; the book is not a metaphysical image so much as
a philosophical analysis which makes use of a metaphysical image' (Murdoch 1999: 48).

La Nausée then offers a rather disturbing and yet appealing image of the
human situation, but it does not offer any solution (Murdoch 1999: 45).
Murdoch looks for Sartre's more positive points in other novels, and in his
writing on literature and philosophy, and finally in his political work.

As a European socialist intellectual with an acute sense of the needs of his
time Sartre wishes to affirm the preciousness of the individual and the possibility of a society which is free and democratic in the traditional liberal
sense of these terms. . . . As a philosopher however he finds himself without
the materials to construct a system which will hold and justify these
values; Sartre believes neither in God nor in Nature nor in History.
What he *does* believe in is Reason . . . Sartre is a rationalist; for him the
supreme virtue is reflective self-awareness. (Murdoch 1999: 105)

This is the dilemma of Sartre that Murdoch is most fascinated by. Sartre wants to defend the preciousness of the individual, but he despises most means to do so: God, Nature, History. The only true value Sartre acknowledges is that of self-reflection.

This individual finds itself on the one hand threatened by the deadening stability of the existence of things, and by people, who will try to make him or her into a thing. In Sartre's world people can only relate by domination or submission. On the other hand, the individual cannot reach any salvation via its reason. Its notion of freedom is contradictory: 'The empty consciousness flickers like a vain fire between the inert petrifying reality which threatens to engulf it and the impossible totality of a stabilised freedom. There is total freedom or total immersion, empty reflexion or silence' (Murdoch 1999: 110–111). The situation is hopeless, but as a Romantic he embraces this hopelessness. 'When in insuperable practical difficulties a sense of "all or nothing" is what *consoles*' (Murdoch 1999: 111; cf. Murdoch 1997: 340–341).

Sartre: Romantic Rationalist expresses Murdoch's fascination, but also her disappointment with Sartre's understanding of human beings. This disappointment she expresses in the work's closing words:

> [Sartre's] inability to write a great novel is a tragic symptom of a situation which afflicts us all. We know that the real lesson to be taught is that the human person is precious and unique; but we seem unable to set it forth except in terms of ideology and abstraction. (Murdoch 1999: 148)

These words, I argued before, have often been quoted as indicative of her own thought. Thus, even though Murdoch becomes more and more critical of existentialism, *La Nausée* cannot easily be discarded as a possibility that did not live up to its expectations. Instead, existentialism slowly comes to occupy her own mind (as she puts it herself when talking about analytical philosophers (Murdoch 1997: 337–338)). Sartre's problem turns out to be her problem. In the first chapter of *Sartre: Romantic Rationalist* she cannot decide whether Roquentin represents everyone, or only philosophers, or even only Sartre's mind. In later writing she has to acknowledge the similarity between Roquentin and various contemporary representations of individuals, including her own. It may still be a philosopher's problem most of all, but it is certainly not just Sartre's.

How profoundly the image of Roquentin has captured Murdoch's imagination is apparent not only from its recurrence until her last work of philosophy, but also in her literary work. There are various allusions to it, often in puns. For example, Jake Donaghue in *Under the Net* comments on parts of

London 'where contingency reaches the point of nausea' (as quoted in Phillips 1991: 47). He is also one of the various main (almost always male) characters and narrators in Murdoch's novels, who do not acknowledge any binding commitment to family or friends. They literally embody this independent existence. Their bodies are remarkably immaterial, hardly affected by time, and without any distinguishing features. These men pride themselves on not having to shave often, on not being bald, nor small, nor fat, thin or large. Charles Arrowby in *The Sea, The Sea* thus contrasts with his cousin James, who 'has to shave twice a day. Sometimes he positively looks dirty' (Murdoch 1978: 173–174). Dirt, in contrast, becomes an almost redeeming feature in Murdoch's novels. One only has to think of the kitchen of her one true saint, Tallis, in *A Fairly Honourable Defeat*. Bradley Pearson in *The Black Prince* prides himself on his clean outlook and Rupert in *A Fairly Honourable Defeat* has not lost his boyish looks, whereas his wife Hilda decidedly shows her age.

Her novels also create imagery in reply to Sartre's, often prior to the systematic refutation in her philosophical writing. Allen, in his 'Two Experiences of Existence: Jean-Paul Sartre and Iris Murdoch', discusses a striking instance. In *The Unicorn* Effingham Cooper, a rather egoistic, 'intelligent and successful civil servant', finds himself at one point trapped in a bog from which there seems no escape and death is near. At the proximity of his death he has a most unusual experience:

Something had been withdrawn, had slipped away from him in the moment of his attention, and that something was simply himself. Perhaps he was dead already, the darkening image of the self forever removed. Yet what was left, for something was surely left, something existed still? It came to him with the simplicity of the simple sum. What was left was everything else, all that was not himself, that object which he had never before seen and upon which he now gazed with the passion of a lover. (Murdoch 1963: 167; also quoted in Allen 1974: 182–183)

Allen considers this image a direct response to that of Roquentin. Where the one experiences reality as something that must be loved, the other's experience of reality is to feel nauseous. Allen points out that neither experience is close to any ordinary form of experience. Their importance he places in the evaluation each of them makes of ordinary experience, reasoning from these extraordinary ones. Allen argues that for Sartre ordinary experience is self-deception, for Murdoch it is serious distortion. For Sartre there is no way out: people are craving for completeness, which can never be obtained without giving up freedom. For Murdoch the inward person needs to be broken down in order to make space for what is outside. This imagery reveals the direction of Murdoch's thought. While maintaining the importance of consciousness she attempts to relate it to a reality independent of it – a relation, moreover, which is beneficial rather than nauseating.

For Murdoch, Sartre's work reveals the problem she faces as both a novelist, concerned with the creation of character, and as a philosopher. Like Sartre, Murdoch is looking for means to 'affirm the preciousness of the individual'. Yet already in the first chapter of *Sartre: Romantic Rationalist*, she doubts if the individual can only be defended through Roquentin's image, and if the individual can only be imagined as Roquentin. With Marcel she wonders in *Sartre: Romantic Rationalist*'s first chapter: 'why ... does Sartre find the contingent over-abundance of the world nauseating rather than glorious?' (Murdoch 1999: 49). In 'The Sublime and the Beautiful Revisited' she writes how existentialism's Totalitarian Man 'is entirely alone. . . . In the world inhabited by Totalitarian Man there are other people, but there are not real contingent separate other people' (Murdoch 1997: 268 and 269). Her answer to this solitude will be to connect the self to reality again, which in these essays is understood as a common sense concept. Murdoch attempts a return to this world, which Sartre found nauseating. Murdoch's on-going discussion with Anglo-Saxon philosophy shows how she tries to introduce consciousness in its relation to reality; how she attempts to retain the (moral) importance existentialism attributes to private deliberation, against a moral philosophy that focuses on observable actions; and how she, unlike existentialism, tries to connect these deliberations to an independent reality. The following discussion of M and D considers what difficulties she encounters in these attempts.

A Mother-in-Law M and her Daughter-in-Law D

The example of M and D has become the emblem of Murdoch's thought, yet it first arose in a specific context, the essay 'The Idea of Perfection' (1964). This text is the first of three essays that together make up *The Sovereignty of Good* (1970), Murdoch's best-known work of philosophy. All three had been previously published individually and were only assembled for the series 'Studies in Ethics and Philosophy of Religion', edited by D.Z. Phillips (Conradi 2001b: 492).[14] In the latter two, 'On "God" and "Good"' (1969) and 'The Sovereignty of Good Over Other Concepts' (1967), Murdoch develops her own moral philosophy around the idea of the Good. The state of contemporary philosophy is briefly and idiosyncratically described in the first few pages of each of the two essays.[15]

A first and obvious difference between 'The Idea of Perfection' and the other two essays is its length. 'The Idea of Perfection' is considerably longer, roughly one and a half times the size of each of the other two. Another distinguishing feature explains this first difference. In 'The Idea of Perfection' Murdoch is constrained by the arguments as well as by the form of argumentation she encounters in the prevalent discussion in moral philosophy. Because of this constraint she finds herself repeatedly unable to pursue her own argument and consequently forced to try bolder, new directions. This time-consuming procedure is replaced by a more concise, idiosyncratic depiction of current moral philosophy in the other two essays.

The on-going dispute in 'The Idea of Perfection' can in the first instance be best characterized by a metaphor Murdoch introduces into the discussion: the metaphor of struggle. Images of struggle are invoked throughout this essay. Thus one finds Murdoch 'mounting an attack upon this heavily fortified position' (Murdoch 1997: 311) or appealing for 'some sort of change of key, some moving of the attack to a different front' (Murdoch 1997: 318). It may be a defining moment when she remarks, in parenthesis: '(There is curiously little place in the other picture for the idea of *struggle*)' (Murdoch 1997: 317, italics in original).[16]

This struggle is to a certain degree decided by temperament, which for Murdoch is a natural ingredient of philosophical debate. She does not mind admitting that it may be temperament which decides whether one is satisfied with a certain argument, 'whether or not we *want* to attack or whether we are content. I am not content' (Murdoch 1997: 311, italics in original).[17] In the first sentence of 'On "God" and "Good"' she even suggests that philosophy is as much about temperament as it is about truth: 'To do philosophy is to explore one's own temperament and yet at the same time to attempt to discover the truth' (Murdoch 1997: 337). The way in which temperament characterizes the dispute in 'The Idea of Perfection' is well illustrated by the image of people protesting and crying out only to receive a cool reply from philosophers (Murdoch 1997: 309). The philosophers' cool reply does not only convey a very different sort of temperament, but also suggests that to them temperament should be of no importance in a philosophical debate.

In 'The Idea of Perfection' Murdoch is discontented with 'current moral philosophy' for two reasons: 'it ignores certain facts and at the same time imposes a single theory which admits of no communication with or escape into rival theories' (Murdoch 1997: 299). Taking her cue from Moore, who answered McTaggart's 'time is unreal' by 'I just had breakfast', Murdoch proposes 'a move back again towards the consideration of simple and obvious facts'. These facts have been 'forgotten or "theorised away"'. Murdoch mentions two such facts: 'the fact that an unexamined life can be virtuous and the fact that love is a central concept in morals', and concludes: 'it must be possible to do justice to both Socrates and the virtuous peasant' (Murdoch 1997: 299–300). Thus, in 'The Idea of Perfection' Murdoch starts an argument against a position that leaves no room for other positions and she does so by returning to certain facts. Talking of facts is indeed a 'bold' thing to do, for in 'The Idea of Perfection' as in other essays Murdoch challenges the strict distinction between fact and value.[18] Murdoch's facts are indeed of an unusual kind. The moral philosophers Murdoch argues against in 'The Idea of Perfection' would not at all recognize as facts those mentioned by Murdoch: 'the fact that an unexamined life can be virtuous and the fact that love is a central concept in morals'.

The position Murdoch introduces against 'current moral philosophy' is often indicated by words like 'simple' and 'obvious'. 'Simple', 'simply', 'obvious', 'surely' are all regularly used, often in opposition to philosophy. So one finds people protesting and crying out against philosophers, when the latter have reasoned away the inner life: '*Surely* there is such a thing as decid-ing and not acting? *Surely* there are *private* decisions? *Surely* there are lots and lots of objects, more or less easily identified, in orbit as it were in inner space?' And even after the cool reply these people maintain that they '*surely* ... *do* have images, talk to [them]selves etc.' (Murdoch 1997: 309–310; emphasis of 'surely' is mine, and of 'private' and of 'do' is Murdoch's).[19]

It is the simple and obvious that likewise inspires the 'rough ordinary' analysis of the example of M and D, 'as yet without justification':

[I]s not the metaphor of vision almost irresistibly suggested to *anyone* who, *without philosophical prejudice*, wishes to describe the situation? Is it not a *natural* metaphor? ... M's activity here, so far from being something very odd and hazy, is something which, in a way, *we* find *exceedingly familiar*. Innumerable novels contain accounts of what such struggles are like. *Anybody* could describe one without being at a loss for words. (Murdoch 1997: 316–317, emphasis added)

With expressions such as 'without philosophical prejudice', 'natural' and 'exceedingly familiar' Murdoch is appealing to some form of common sense that all should recognize from life or from innumerable novels.

The reference to 'innumerable novels' is noteworthy here. It calls back to mind how important literature is for Murdoch's thought, as discussed in the first part of this chapter. Novels are opposed to philosophy, and likened to the familiar. Somebody looking for a way to describe M and D would natu-rally use the metaphor of vision, Murdoch maintains. Innumerable novels provide vocabulary for anyone to describe the situation differently from the analysis of philosophy.

The supporters of simple and obvious facts in 'The Idea of Perfection' dissent from 'ideally rational man'. He represents the kind of moral philosophy Murdoch intends to challenge. She assembles his image from two works by Hampshire: *Thought and Action* and 'Disposition and Memory'. The term 'ideally rational man' is taken from the latter (Murdoch 1997: 303; cf. Hampshire 1972: 176). He is introduced with a considerable amount of quotation, from which it is possible to pull out ideally rational man's main features. First, his intentions should be clear. Murdoch writes: '[Hampshire] utters in relation to intention the only explicit "ought" in his philosophy. We ought to know what we are doing' (Murdoch 1997: 304). In 'The Darkness of Practical Reasoning' and 'On "God" and "Good" ' she argues that it is indeed possible for Hampshire to maintain this requirement, for he considers it always possible to take a step back and reconsider the situation (Murdoch 1997: 194; 340). Second, the thoughts and actions of 'ideally rational man' are directed to what is overtly observable. Reality is thus defined as 'potentially open to different observers'. This observable world of facts is clearly distinguished from the value one may attach to it. This distinction leads to the third point. Decisions are made by the will, which is isolated from reason, belief and emotions. More than once Murdoch quotes Hampshire's 'I identify myself with my will' (Murdoch 1997: 303, 304–305 and 328). For 'ideally rational man' as for Ordinary Language Man from 'The Sublime and the Beautiful Revisited' any daydreaming or musing has no meaning if it is not expressed in words or actions. Morality is reduced to choice. Ordinary Language Man observes the facts, reasons the values and chooses (cf. Murdoch 1997: 267). Both 'ideally rational man' and Ordinary Language Man are decidedly alone, surrounded by a world and a language that has no secrets for them. Other people do not exist other than as similar rational agents (Murdoch 1997: 268).

What Murdoch is most concerned with in 'The Idea of Perfection' is the (moral) absence of the inner life. Murdoch's criticism is thus extended to the philosophy of mind that sustains the moral philosophy (Murdoch 1997: 300). In this philosophy of mind the inner life is, if not insignificant daydreaming, no more than a shadow of the public life. The idea of a private certainty, as for example Descartes' *cogito*, is not only of no use, it is not even there (Murdoch 1997: 307). It is discarded in favour of an understanding of a concept as a public structure. This understanding of meaning is lucidly illustrated by the concept of red: 'the inner picture is necessarily irrelevant and the possession of the concept is a public skill. What matters is whether

I stop at the traffic lights, and not my colour imagery or absence of it' (Murdoch 1997: 307).

Of all the different objections Murdoch formulates against this position I focus on those against the argument that she calls 'the most radical argument, the key-stone ... the argument to the effect that mental concepts must be analysed genetically and so the inner must be thought of as parasitic upon the outer' (Murdoch 1997: 306; cf. Hampshire 1972: 167ff.).[20] It is this argument that makes the position so difficult to challenge. Murdoch describes how it has originated in the *Philosophical Investigations*, but was then further developed by 'Hampshire, Hare, Ayer, Ryle and others' (Murdoch 1997: 308; cf. 311) in a way that is not found in Wittgenstein's own work. According to the genetic argument all concepts are learnt only in public situations. 'The structure of the concept is its public structure, which is established by coinciding procedures in public situations' (Murdoch 1997: 307). In this line of argument the inner life is stripped of all relevance for determining the meaning of concepts and because this is so, Murdoch argues, 'it has been too hastily assumed that something else is not there' (Murdoch 1997: 307).

Recapturing the inner life proves to be difficult (Murdoch 1997: 309–311). After her first attempts Murdoch expresses the need for an object that we can all look at. She suggests that she might have used an example other than that of M and D, namely that of a ritual. A ritual, just as the example used, begs the question of the inner life or of what is extra to public words and gestures: whether being sorry adds to saying one is, or whether one is repentant when one says so, or beats one's chest. Murdoch, however, does not pursue this religious example, because it 'might be felt to raise special difficulties'. Instead she turns to something 'more ordinary and everyday'.[21]

The example is well known. A mother M is unhappy with her son's choice of a bride. She considers her daughter-in-law D 'quite a good-hearted girl, but while not exactly common yet certainly unpolished and lacking in dignity and refinement'. The dislike is considerable. It does not just concern D's behaviour, but includes even her accent and her sense of dress. M does not show her aversion, but instead she 'is a very "correct" person, [and] behaves beautifully to the girl throughout, not allowing her real opinion to appear in any way'. Time passes, and for one reason or another (emigration or death) D has disappeared from M's life. Yet, M does not sit down to nurture her grudge. Instead, she comes round to consider D again, and to find that D is 'not vulgar but refreshingly simple, not undignified but spontaneous, not noisy but gay, not tiresomely juvenile but delightfully youthful, and so on' (Murdoch 1997: 312–313).

This engaging imagery, introduced by Murdoch as an example, has obtained in the secondary literature the status of the emblem of Murdoch's philosophy, in particular but not exclusively in Antonaccio's *Picturing the Human*. Antonaccio calls it 'a prominent example . . . of [a] kind of conceptual analysis in the form of "pictures" and images of human existence in order to analyze moral identity in relation to the good' and 'a particularly rich illustration of many of Murdoch's complex theoretical points' (Antonaccio 2000: 22 and 24). The image is of great significance in Antonaccio's work. She distinguishes different aspects in which the image is different from Hamsphire's 'ideally rational man' (Antonaccio 2000: 88–95). However, by using the terms 'example' and 'illustration' she allows that the image may be omitted.

I shall argue that the image cannot be omitted, because it not only illustrates Murdoch's arguments, but it also shows their difficulties. It is indeed true that the musings and personal thoughts cannot be omitted. The image is thus formulated that the inner life is *per definition* of importance for moral philosophy and the change happening within that inner life is *per definition* good. Whatever it is that is happening it is only happening within the inner life. M's change of view is not noticeable, for M has behaved correctly throughout. Neither is there any observable external cause that encourages or forces M to change her image of D. The change is not instigated by D or by anyone else. Murdoch attributes the change to M being 'an intelligent and well-intentioned person, capable of self-criticism, capable of giving careful and just *attention* to an object which confronts her' (Murdoch 1997: 313). In an internal monologue M corrects herself and decides to look again. The words 'intelligent', 'well-intentioned', etc. are deliberately chosen to convey that the change of view should be considered as good. Murdoch explicitly asks her readers to think of the change in that way. She acknowledges that it may be very difficult to decide whether M's change of mind is proper or not 'in real life, and this is of interest'. Is it delusion or love that moves M to do so? Murdoch holds that she has created a picture where love would provide the appropriate description (Murdoch 1997: 313).

Murdoch adds specific claims 'to ensure that whatever is in question as *happening* happens entirely in M's mind' (Murdoch 1997: 312). The couple has moved away, or D has died. However, for the analytical philosophers at whom this argument is directed, these claims make the example irrelevant for moral philosophy. The refutation follows immediately, and Murdoch characteristically presents it as if in a dialogue. A philosopher, she suggests, can argue either that there is no inner life and since there is no change in the outer life either, it is difficult to speak of any change at all. Or, there is some form of inner life, but for this form of inner life to regain meaning and not to be just 'the charmed and habitual rehearsal of phrases' (Murdoch 1997: 315) one needs the outer world. On her own M cannot give meaning to what she is doing or give meaning to the words she speaks to herself (Murdoch 1997: 313–316; cf. Antonaccio 2000: 88). This setback leads Murdoch to exclaim miserably that '[t]his is one of those exasperating moments in philosophy when one seems to be being relentlessly prevented from saying something which one is irresistibly impelled to say' (Murdoch 1997: 316).

Murdoch counters this exasperation by stating 'in a rough and ordinary way and as yet without justification' what she thinks to be the case. The example shows M to be making moral progress and her thoughts are part of her being: 'one feels impelled to say something like: M's activity is peculiarly *her own*. ... M could not *do this* thing in conversation with another person' (Murdoch 1997: 316–317, emphasis in original). Against analytical philosophy's interest limited to the observable Murdoch posits the importance of the inner life and of private deliberation. In order to strengthen her argument and the private character of morality she suggests the absence of any other person. 'M could not *do this* thing in conversation with another person.' Murdoch dismisses even D: 'the young couple have emigrated or . . . D is now dead'. Yet, at this point, the example becomes incongruous. For, when Murdoch later remarks that 'M observes D' (Murdoch 1997: 313), 'M *looks* at D, she attends to D, she focuses her attention' (Murdoch 1997: 317), should it be surmised that this too happens entirely in M's mind? D – the object of attention – has emigrated or died. Whom then is M looking at?

The lasting absence of D does not impede M's attempts to change her thoughts on D. Yet, the stipulation occasions a surprising contrast to the language of vision and attention. M looks at D, but D is not actually present. The contrast arises again when Murdoch later connects the idea of perfection and the idea of the individual: 'Love is knowledge of the individual. M confronted with D has an endless task' (Murdoch 1997: 821). Murdoch also mentions, referring to Weil, the notion of attention, 'the idea of a just and loving gaze directed upon an individual reality. I believe this to be the characteristic and proper mark of the active moral agent' (Murdoch 1997: 327).

The supposition of D's absence is to suit the arguments against the analytical philosophers, as it makes evident that there is absolutely no change but in M's mind. Yet, it creates an unusual picture of this change. Without any external prompting or direction M conceives of a better picture of D. If D had been there all along, it is easy to picture how M might have changed her mind for a variety of reasons: M may feel obliged to defend her son's choice against neighbours or colleagues; both women could get more used to one another; M accepts the situation out of love for her son, etc. Similarly, in D's absence, it is possible to envision external reasons for M's change of mind. However, the claims put upon this image exclude these possibilities. What M is doing is not perceived or influenced by anyone. It is a purely individual activity. M changes her mind to obtain a more realistic picture in complete solitude.

It can be argued that the difficulty of imagining this change of mind is because it is rare. Recalling the depressing picture Murdoch has of human beings, it should not be surprising that they rarely imagine something as extraordinary as changing one's mind without any external compulsion to do so. The difficulty of envisioning this change of mind does not entail the impossibility of doing so. Yet, Murdoch has added extra claims in order to meet the philosophical argument. What M thinks is *per definition* of importance and the change is *per definition* good, for if not the picture would no longer fit the philosophical argument. The absence of any observable change necessitates the conclusion that the change must have been in M's mind. However, at the same time Murdoch also supposes the absence of any reality of other people surrounding M. M is a lonely individual, and in her loneliness more like Roquentin than Murdoch would like her to be.

Against this reading of M and D it may be argued that too much weight is given to D's absence. As a detail of the picture it receives too much emphasis. Murdoch is after all not concerned with D in this example of M and D, but with M's inner life. She needs an example to challenge the arguments of analytical philosophy and to introduce a rich and important understanding of inner life into the philosophical debate. D is absent only as guarantee that whatever is happening happens in M's mind alone.

Yet, I would argue that the noted difficulty of introducing an inner life in relation to an independent reality is not just reflected in this detail, but instead characterizes the entire essay. The image of M and D reflects the difficulty Murdoch has when trying to refute the arguments of analytical philosophy and to introduce the facts she mentions at the beginning of the essay. Against their exasperating refutation of her arguments Murdoch adjusts her own arguments in order to make them more decisive. She attempts to convince her adversaries of the importance of the inner life by making sure that whatever is happening happens in M's mind alone. Yet, this attempt to present a conclusive argumentation also introduces imagery that surprisingly contrasts with the central imagery of vision and attention.

Earlier I argued that 'The Idea of Perfection' is very different from the other two essays in *The Sovereignty of Good* in its representation of contemporary philosophy. I pointed out that in this essay Murdoch is more constrained by the arguments as well as the form of argumentation encountered in the analytical tradition. My reading of M and D offers additional insight into this difference by arguing that in her involvement with the analytical tradition Murdoch feels compelled to present her own argument as conclusive. In contrast in the other essays, she significantly recognizes the limitations of her own arguments. Thus, in 'On "God" and "Good"' she admits that 'Philosophical argument is almost always inconclusive' (Murdoch 1997: 360). In order to discuss her facts it may turn out to be necessary for Murdoch to give up the desire to provide the final conquering argumentation.

This absence of D is thus not incidental, but may be understood to point to a more general philosophical difficulty. In encountering this difficulty Murdoch is not alone. Just as M does not think any better of D until D is gone, so many a philosopher only considers the tiresome juvenile reality that is the real topic of study. Only in the retirement of the study can this reality be valued. This does not imply that everything done there is useless. One would be cynical to suggest that what M does is of no use. Yet, M's example also urges towards leaving this study and perhaps accepting that philosophical argument in the face of reality can no longer be definite.

Conclusion

This chapter ends with a solitary mother-in-law and started with Murdoch's criticism of the lonely individual she encountered in both analytical and existentialist philosophy. I argued that Murdoch positions her understanding of character, as found in novels from the nineteenth century, against the 'flimsy personality' of analytical and existentialist philosophy. The references to character and to literature are considered not as illustration or example, but as a structuring principle in Murdoch's thought. In doing so, I show its indebtedness to Le Doeuff's notion of the philosophical imaginary. The image of the nineteenth century novel allows Murdoch to express central values for which she does not have philosophical arguments, the most important of these being that the inner life is central to morality. Using words like 'simple' and 'surely' emphasizes the belief that these straightforward values usually need no other explanation. It turns out to be indeed difficult to find defeating arguments against contemporary analytical philosophy. The image of M and D, which is central to that argument, shows the intrinsic difficulty Murdoch encounters: to argue for the importance of reality from a single starting-point.

Murdoch is one of the few philosophers in the past century who have tried to cross the gap between Anglo-Saxon and continental traditions in philosophy. Yet, even though Murdoch will criticize both analytical and existentialist philosophy more and more in the same argument, I consider her criticism to be directed against the former more than the latter. Murdoch encountered existentialism only after her studies in Oxford, and when later again teaching in Oxford she was one of very few philosophers interested in it. Existentialism first excited Murdoch for its interest in literature, in moral value and in consciousness. All these topics were of limited importance to the analytical philosophy she encountered in Oxford. However, already in her book on Sartre, Murdoch is critical of existentialism and aware of possible difficulties. The most prominent of those she notes in the last lines of *Sartre: Romantic Rationalist*. Murdoch considers Sartre unable to defend the preciousness and uniqueness of the individual other than 'in terms of ideology and abstraction'. Existentialism shows itself unable to remedy analytical philosophy and in Murdoch's vocabulary the term becomes synonymous with some of the failures of all contemporary philosophy.

I have not considered whether the values Murdoch finds in the nineteenth-century novel are indeed the values 'we' consider 'ordinary'. The persistently growing interest in her work could prove its commonality to some extent, yet it is impossible simply to accept the values Murdoch finds in the nineteenth-century novel. They are not that simple. However, to pursue this line of thought may divert from Murdoch's achievement. Even if Murdoch's notion of ordinary is not everyone's, it should be possible to express this position in philosophical argument. Murdoch found that she could not as long as the genetic argument was considered invincible. So, Murdoch does not only introduce new values into philosophical debate, but also makes it reflect on its own limitations.

Imagination

Introduction

This chapter considers the notions of imagination and fantasy as in a way the successors to Murdoch's understanding of character. Imagination and fantasy express similar concerns for the moral importance of the inner life in relation to a reality independent of it. Imagination is not a notion foreign to the history of philosophy. Murdoch becomes interested in imagination and fantasy when writing on Kant's aesthetics from 1959 onwards, but her reading of his work is highly dependent on her understanding of literature and character. Especially in the earlier texts she presents her understanding of imagination and of art as in a way opposed to Kant's. In *Metaphysics as a Guide to Morals* the reading of Kant is augmented by a discussion of Plato.

Of the different texts considering imagination I regard the longer depiction in Murdoch's last and largest work of philosophy, *Metaphysics as a Guide to Morals*, as the most important one. My discussion concentrates on this text, but often returns to the various, usually brief, earlier appearances of imagination in her philosophical writing. These earlier texts are indispensable for understanding *Metaphysics as a Guide to Morals*. Throughout the chapter there are implied references to ideas discussed more extensively before. This I have found to be characteristic of Murdoch's philosophical thinking. Murdoch habitually appropriates ideas in telling imagery, short phrases or even in a single term. From these texts I compose the different aspects of the *animal imaginationale*, the 'fantasising imaginative animals' Murdoch considers the human being to be. Again, the interpretation has to deal with reading a number of different texts written over a period of more than thirty years, texts that are moreover concerned with different topics. With the possible exception of the texts based on the 1982 Gifford lectures, Murdoch is not interested in imagination *per se*. The notion of imagination and its counterpart fantasy appear in texts concerned with art, art criticism and art theory, as well as moral philosophy.

This chapter consists of three parts. The first part introduces the distinction between imagination and fantasy, but as yet without much reference to

Kant or Plato. Instead, it explains the connection between Murdoch's understanding of character and of imagination and fantasy. From this discussion I proceed to examining Murdoch's apprehension of the two philosophers from whom in *Metaphysics as a Guide to Morals* she retrieves the different aspects of imagination and fantasy, Kant and Plato.

Imagination and Fantasy

The distinction between imagination and fantasy is found in Chapter 11 of *Metaphysics as a Guide to Morals*, at a third into this chapter. It marks a significant shift. The preceding part discusses Kant and Plato, to which the distinction forms the conclusion. The remainder of the chapter is an amalgam of topics, ranging from a discussion of the will to the relation between aesthetics and morals, the difference between moral and religious experience, and love. There is no obvious structure to this second part.

The pivotal position of imagination and fantasy in this chapter reflects its position in Murdoch's oeuvre. Its appearance is often brief, but crucial. The distinction first appears in articles on Kant and art, dating back to the late fifties and early sixties: 'The Sublime and the Good' (1959), 'The Sublime and the Beautiful Revisited' (1959) and 'Against Dryness' (1961).[1] It is next found in a more established mode in 'The Sovereignty of Good Over Other Concepts' (1967), 'Philosophy and Literature: An Interview with Bryan Magee' (1977), 'Art is the Imitation of Nature' (1978) and finally in one of the Gifford lectures, published first as 'Ethics and the Imagination' (1987) and lastly as the eleventh chapter in *Metaphysics as a Guide to Morals* (1992).

Murdoch often presents the distinction between imagination and fantasy as a *theoretical* distinction, which would be much more difficult to find in any clear form in actual texts or works of art. In *Metaphysics as a Guide to Morals* she expresses the need for 'two words for two concepts', and instantly questions the distinction she makes – in the dialogue-like style so typical for this work. It is as if her idea is interrupted by someone's interjection:

> To mark distances we need for purposes of discussion, two words for two concepts: a distinction between egoistic *fantasy* and liberated truth-seeking creative *imagination*. Can there not be high evil fantasising forms of creative imaginative activity? A search for candidates will, I think, tend to reinforce at least the usefulness of a distinction between 'fantasy' as mechanical, egoistic, untruthful, and 'imagination' as truthful and free. (Murdoch 1993: 321, emphasis in original)

In the interview with Magee she admits that 'creative imagination and obsessive fantasy may be very close almost indistinguishable forces in the mind of the writer' (Murdoch 1997: 11). Murdoch's doubts caution against ready acceptance of the distinction. It may be useful for the discussion, but it is not easily recognized in a writer's mind or in any particular text. It should not come as a surprise, then, that even though Spear in her introduction suggests that '[t]he theme of fantasy versus imagination is a recurrent one in her non-fiction and is a significant index to an understanding of her fiction', she does not return to this remark when discussing the different novels (Spear 1995: 9).

In *Metaphysics as a Guide to Morals* fantasy and imagination are distinguished from one another by terms like 'egoistic' on the one side and 'liberated truth-seeking creative' on the other; 'mechanical, egoistic, untruthful' are opposed to 'truthful and free'. To contrast her distinction to Coleridge's fancy and imagination Murdoch explains that she conceives of 'two active faculties: one somewhat mechanically generating narrowly banal false pictures (the ego as all-powerful), and the other freely and creatively exploring the world, moving towards the expression and elucidation (and in art celebration) of what is true and deep' (Murdoch 1993: 321). The distinction is consistently presented in *moral* terms. *Bad* fantasy is opposed to *good* imagination.[2] Through fantasy people only look after themselves, while imagination looks at the world and is cheerfully described as 'creative ... liberated ... truth-seeking ... elucidation ... celebration'. Fantasy is called mechanical, whereas imagination is connected to creativity and exploration.[3]

The description in *Metaphysics as a Guide to Morals* explores the distinction between imagination and fantasy through opposing concepts. For a more straightforward description of imagination one has to go back to 'The Darkness of Practical Reasoning' (1966), a review of Hampshire's *Freedom of the Individual*. This article differs from the others in which imagination is mentioned, in that it is one of the last articles in which Murdoch closely engages with a philosophical text from the analytical tradition. Against Hampshire and much of the analytical tradition Murdoch prefers art to science as a model for philosophy, and *imagination* to the *will* as the focus of moral philosophy.[4] The article shows how these preferences considerably change the outlook of philosophy. Most importantly, there no longer is 'just a world of "facts" ' (Murdoch 1997: 199).

Murdoch introduces imagining as 'something which we all *do* a great deal of the time'. She understands imagination, she claims, 'in a sense more like its normal one' – calling to mind the many appearances of 'simple' and 'surely' throughout 'The Idea of Perfection'. Imagination is 'a type of reflection on people, events, etc., which builds detail, adds colour, conjures up possibilities in ways that go beyond what could be said to be factual'. Murdoch also and immediately introduces the bad form of this kind of reflection: ' "fantasy or wishful thinking" '. Murdoch objects to Hampshire's relegation of imagination 'to the passive side of the mind, regarding it as an isolated non-responsible faculty' (Murdoch 1997: 198). For Murdoch, in contrast, imagination and fantasy are central. They affect all cognition, including perception, so that no one lives in a world of 'facts', but always in a world constructed by imagination and fantasy. Again, to claim as much is to claim nothing special. 'To be a human being is to know more than one can prove, to conceive of a reality which goes "beyond the facts" in these familiar and natural ways' (Murdoch 1997: 199).

For Murdoch, then, imagination and fantasy are all-encompassing, and 'it is false to suggest that we could, even in principle, "purge" the world we confront of these personal elements. Nor is there any reason why we should' (Murdoch 1997: 199). Human beings create their own world, through imagination and fantasy. The central distinction is between these two notions – imagination and fantasy, the good and the bad – rather than between imagination and facts. And yet, Murdoch habitually uses words like 'reality' or 'world' to explain her moral ideal. This world cannot be an impersonal collection of facts, nor a purely personal creation. What it *is* often remains implicit.

In 'On "God" and "Good" ', for instance, Murdoch writes:

> morality, goodness, is a form of realism. The idea of a really good man living in a private dream world seems unacceptable. Of course a good man may be infinitely eccentric, but he must know *certain things* about his surroundings, *most obviously* the existence of other people and their claims. (Murdoch 1997: 347, emphasis added)

So, the good man must be aware of his surroundings, but what are these 'certain things'? What things? Surely not facts? Murdoch's subsequent explanation comes in the form of an image: 'Rilke said of Cézanne that he did not paint "I like it", he painted "There it is". This is not easy, and requires, in art or morals, a discipline' (Murdoch 1997: 348).[5] 'There it is', but Cézanne's paintings are not photorealistic. One is here reminded too of the discussion of M and D where Murdoch argues that 'M confronted with D has an endless task' (Murdoch 1997: 321). Again, Murdoch does not explain whether D is *really* 'vulgar' or 'refreshingly simple', 'undignified' or 'spontaneous', 'noisy' or 'gay', 'tiresomely juvenile' or 'delightfully youthful', etc.

For Murdoch, the distinction between imagination and fantasy is 'obvious', even though it is not 'easy'. As an obvious distinction, it is explained by example rather than extended argument. What imagination is can be learnt most obviously from examples of great art. Even though imagination and fantasy are not limited to the arts, but found in 'intellectual disciplines and in the enjoyment of art and nature' (Murdoch 1997: 374), art nevertheless offers for Murdoch the most prominent examples. The paintings of Cézanne and Velasquez, the music of Bach and the works of Shakespeare show imagination in its most excellent form.[6] The references to the works of these artists are general and rarely explained in detail.[7] Rather they are introduced by an imperative: *consider*: 'Consider what we learn from contemplating the characters of Shakespeare or Tolstoy or the paintings of Velasquez or Titian' (Murdoch 1997: 353; cf. 348). Murdoch refrains here from an explanation by means of a discussion of artistic devices. Her argument suggests a shared understanding of the works of these artists. This suggestion of immediacy and collectivity when reading literature is even stronger in the first of the two chapters on consciousness in *Metaphysics as a Guide to Morals*. Here Murdoch quotes the pagoda passage from James' *Golden Bowl* and concludes: 'How is it done? Well, like that and in innumerable other ways. Do we understand? Yes, of course, we follow, in context, these descriptions of states of consciousness with no difficulty' (Murdoch 1993: 171).

This last example shows not only Murdoch's appeal to immediate understanding, but also the close connection between imagination and literary criticism, or indeed how the distinction between imagination and fantasy proceeds from her literary criticism. In an interview with Magee, Murdoch notes that literature may be criticized in 'a purely formal way', but is 'more often . . . criticised for being in some sense untruthful'. Such common criticism uses words like 'sentimental', 'pretentious', 'self-indulgent', 'trivial'. In other words, the object of criticism is a work of fantasy, not imagination (Murdoch 1997: 11). Habitually, Murdoch presents her ideas as sensible and nothing extraordinary. Literature may be criticized in one way, but it is *'more often* . . . criticised for being . . . untruthful'. To discuss art in terms of true and false is, Murdoch suggests, nothing extraordinary.

Whether this form of criticism is indeed common is debatable. Literary critics have pointed out its idiosyncrasies, and argued that it is not so much common criticism, but Platonic – only common to natural Platonists. Thus, Bronzwaer argues, for Murdoch, as for Plato, art can guide to a better understanding of beauty, of truth, and ultimately goodness. At the same time, however, (written) words will fail to express what is beautiful, what is true, and what is good (Bronzwaer 1988: 56ff.). The aesthetic ideal is never expressed in the text, but always looms beyond the text. So, even though it may be common to judge literature in terms of true or false, it may not be possible to identify the truthfulness. This would certainly explain why Murdoch urges her readers to *consider* the works of art, without much instruction.

For Wood, this Platonic aesthetics means that Murdoch is even somewhat impatient with actual works of art. Murdoch does not develop her aesthetics through close engagement with individual works, he argues. On the contrary, before developing her aesthetics she already knows that Shakespeare is 'the greatest of all artists. ... Shakespeare represents the Good'.[8] This ideal explains for Wood Murdoch's 'lack of interest, as a novelist, in surfaces, in the pigments of reality ... It may illuminate why she appears to attend so little, as a novelist, to her prose, which seems good only by accident, and is often careless'(Wood 1999: 182–183). Indeed, for Wood her philosophical stance has regretably hindered her development as a novelist. Her novels, he argues, are moral exercises doomed to fail (Wood 1999: 175ff.). Only when it shows its failure to express the ideal can great art point 'in the direction of the good and [be] more valuable to the moralist as an auxiliary than dangerous as an enemy' (Murdoch 1997: 454)[9].

The comparison with Plato shows why the distinction between imagination and fantasy is both 'obvious', and not 'easy'. Like Plato Murdoch does not have a very positive understanding of human beings. People rarely use their imagination. To paint 'There it is', Murdoch argues, requires discipline. To consider one's daughter-in-law as 'refreshingly simple' rather than 'vulgar' requires endless effort. Even though, for Plato as for Murdoch, all human beings are endowed with the capacity to distinguish good from bad, that does not mean that human beings use this capacity. Moreover, it is difficult if not impossible to put the distinction into words. Murdoch is puzzled about the passage in which the good man, in Plato's famous myth, has come out of the cave and is finally able to look at the sun. She admits she has 'never been sure what to make of this part of the myth'. Murdoch concludes: 'Perhaps indeed only the good man knows what [it would be like to look at the sun]; or perhaps to look at the sun is to be gloriously dazzled and to see nothing' (Murdoch 1997: 357). Reality, then, in Murdoch's writing is both what one ought *most obviously* to know and what one can only know with great difficulty, if at all. It is not easily comprehensible, yet the good man '*must know certain things* about his surroundings, *most obviously* the existence of other people and their claims'. Given the unlikely experience of looking at the sun, reality means for Murdoch that the moment one thinks one sees the sun, perception and thinking should be mistrusted. The notion of reality is a reminder that whatever it is that we talk or think about, it is more complex, subtler than theories and words can convey. Whatever is *too* neat, *too* clear, should be mistrusted. At the same time, it is obvious that reality is what one should want to know. The difficulty in understanding should not keep one from trying.

Murdoch then presents her understanding of imagination and fantasy as nothing extraordinary, but rather something all virtuous peasants, saints and mothers of large families have known all along. They obviously know the distinction between imagination and fantasy, while others may learn it from contemplating Tolstoy or Shakespeare or from learning a language or a craft. The contemplation of art, which gives rise to the distinction between imagination and fantasy, Murdoch considers her readers able to recognize. It is, however, not an easy distinction to appropriate. It is not easy to use imagination rather than fantasy. This combination of at once being obvious and difficult is also evinced by the notion of reality that distinguishes good imagination from bad fantasy. This notion implies a permanent conflict between the two, where fantasy stops at egoistic imagery and imagination constantly moves on. Imagination and fantasy thus present an understanding of moral philosophy as a constant process of change or, as Murdoch puts it, of moral pilgrimage.

Kant: Imagination in the Small Corner of Art

These notions of imagination and fantasy are then important within Murdoch's moral philosophy. 'The concept of imagination is', she claims, 'an essential one' (Murdoch 1993: 322). In different texts Murdoch suggests that the distinction between imagination and fantasy is not connected to any contemplation of other philosophers. For example, in a discussion of Kant's *Critique of Judgment* the distinction is thus introduced: 'Let me now briefly and dogmatically state what I take to be, in opposition to Kant's view, the true view of the matter' (Murdoch: 1997: 215).

For Murdoch, it is important to emphasize how ordinary her moral ideal is. She often points out how philosophers have complicated ordinary understanding of moral issues. However, it should not be assumed that her philosophy does not relate at all to other philosophy. In *Metaphysics as a Guide to Morals* in particular, the distinction between imagination and fantasy arises from reflection upon similar distinctions made by other thinkers. Here, she describes her indebtedness to two thinkers, Kant and Plato. Indeed, it is not until *Metaphysics as a Guide to Morals* that one can fully appreciate how the development of the notions of imagination and fantasy also depends on Murdoch's idiosyncratic reading of Kant and Plato. My interpretation of this complex text focuses on its literary devices and imagery. In order to do so, it follows the text closely. In thus reading the text, a complicated

interchange between philosophy and literature appears. Murdoch acknowledges the importance of various philosophers, Kant and Plato in particular,
yet reads them with her understanding of literature constantly in mind.

Murdoch often returns to Kant as a thinker who, as she once put it, 'was
marvellously near the mark' or who 'followed a sound instinct but, in my
view, looked in the wrong place' (see respectively Murdoch 1997: 216 and
368). In Kant's philosophy Murdoch locates the presence of many aspects
of contemporary thought that she disputes. Numerous examples may be
given here and her imagery is not always gentle: 'Kant's man had already
received a glorious incarnation nearly a century earlier in the work of
Milton: his proper name is Lucifer' (Murdoch 1997: 366). Yet, Murdoch
considers Kant only partly to blame for the ideas that have ensued from his
work. She also returns to it to pursue his 'sound instincts'. This dual attitude
towards Kant's philosophy (as well as the slightly condescending remarks)
one encounters also in the chapter on imagination.

At the end of the few pages devoted to Kant in this chapter of *Metaphysics
as a Guide to Morals* Murdoch writes:

> How flexible can a deep concept be? is a founding question of philosophy.
> Kant, in his precision, is careful not to demand too much of the concept of
> imagination. He distinguishes the empirical imagination, which sponta-
> neously yet 'mechanically' prepares a sensuous manifold for subjection to
> the synthetic *a priori* and empirical concepts of the understanding, but
> which is not independently creative or aesthetically sensible, from the aes-
> thetic imagination which is spontaneous and free and able to create a
> 'second nature'. But are 'fine art' and 'genius' as described by Kant
> really such a small corner of human faculty and experience? The concept
> of genius itself emerges from an appreciation of the deep and omnipresent
> operation of imagination in human life. (Murdoch 1993: 316)

How flexible can the concept of imagination be? Perhaps, Murdoch suggests, more flexible than she believes Kant allows for. Such flexibility of
deep concepts is not found in the 'mechanical' working Kant attributes to
the empirical imagination, or in the small corner to which Kant directs the
aesthetic imagination.[10] It must be Murdoch then, and not Kant, who concludes that the 'concept of genius itself emerges from an appreciation of the
deep and omnipresent operation of imagination in human life'.

Murdoch observes a friction between Kant's 'precision' and imagination's possibilities. In his precision she understands Kant to place upon
imagination different restrictions. To the empirical imagination Kant
assigns a confined role in understanding. It plays a crucial but restricted –

'mechanic' Murdoch calls it – role in the process of acquiring knowledge. Only to aesthetic imagination does he allow independent creativity and aesthetic sensibility, as it is strictly severed from knowledge and morality. Murdoch questions these limitations in the first few pages of the chapter.

Murdoch's idiosyncratic, 'literary' position first shows in her reading of Kant's empirical imagination. She quickly diverges from other interpretations, even though she also begins, as they do, by considering the empirical imagination.[11] The empirical imagination, in Murdoch's words, 'spontaneously yet "mechanically" prepares a sensuous manifold for subjection to the synthetic *a priori* and empirical concepts of the understanding'. It is, as Murdoch points out, 'a mediator between sense perception and concepts, something between sense and thought'.[12] Significantly, she does not pay much attention to the different tasks assigned to the empirical imagination, or its distinction from the transcendental imagination. She does not mention the epistemological problems Kant's notion of imagination is commonly understood to solve (i.e. the recognition of particular objects as such, as well as the recognition of an individual through time). It may be surmised that she is not so much concerned with the questions Kant asks, as with her own. This supposition is supported by textual evidence. The distinction between transcendental imagination and empirical imagination, as well as the subsequent paragraph on Hume, are later additions to this chapter.[13] The addition has, however, not resulted in major changes in the remainder of the text, in its arguments or conclusions.[14]

On reflection, it should not be surprising that for Murdoch the distinction between empirical and transcendental imagination does not matter as much as it does for Kant. Transcendental for Kant designates the necessary or *a priori* part of knowledge. In *The Critique of Pure Reason* Kant is concerned with the synthetic *a priori* rather than the *a posteriori* part of human understanding, i.e., with the possibility of knowledge that is both necessary and universal, yet not analytical (Kant *Critique of Pure Reason*, B X). For Murdoch, in contrast, necessary knowledge is a distant if not unachievable goal. It is never universal, but always particular. The difference between Kant's and Murdoch's positions is perhaps best grasped from the examples they use. Murdoch's understanding of necessary knowledge is to be found in a mother directing her attention to her daughter-in-law in order to truly perceive her. A well-known example of Kant's necessary knowledge is the proposition that every change has a cause.[15] Thus, the distinction between the transcendental and empirical imagination, where the one provides 'an empty pattern or schematic form' and the second 'sensuously bodied schemata' (Murdoch 1992: 308), difficult even for Kant, disappears in Murdoch's text.[16]

Murdoch adopts the central place Kant attributes to imagination in the understanding, but she also adds significant changes. Her reading of Kant, while disregarding some of the commonly discussed arguments, introduces its own imagery. Most significantly, Murdoch's concern with imagination is expressed in the returning image of a 'barrier'. Kant's transcendental imagination she describes 'as a power of spontaneous synthesis operating at the transcendental barrier of consciousness'. Murdoch notes the disagreement about the exact working of the transcendental imagination, and hesitates to accept a notion of imagination that is held behind a transcendental or unconscious barrier. The direction of her own thoughts is then revealed – again – in the use of the term 'simply': 'Is it misleading *simply* to read the conscious activity back into the unconscious (transcendental) activity?' (Murdoch 1992: 308–309, emphasis added).

Murdoch introduces an understanding of imagination whose spontaneous operation in understanding does not remain entirely unaffected by any conscious operation of the imagination. She attempts to understand imagination's

> unconscious or transcendental 'spontaneity' ... figuratively upon analogy. We can attempt to give sense to the idea, as we extend and modify the conception of a barrier or network (or set of 'schemata'), in terms of empirical concepts, and (now also) of language as a, to some extent consciously manipulable, experiential threshold. (Murdoch 1993: 309)

So, Murdoch attempts to lower the *barrier* until it is no more than a *threshold*. This imagery reveals a distinctive position. The impersonal method of assembly is not entirely closed off for the individual, yet neither is it entirely in his or her control.[17]

Murdoch acknowledges that for Kant these are dangerous thoughts, as they introduce imagination into Kant's purely rational world of morality. The notion of imagination is 'too double-sided a concept, too much like a kind of feeling, to be allowed (by Kant) near the essence of morality' (Murdoch 1993: 310). Yet, Murdoch is not convinced that Kant's understanding of transcendental imagination actually does that, i.e. that it keeps imagination away from morality. Echoing Nietzsche's criticism in *Beyond Good and Evil*, Murdoch remarks: 'One might almost say that "imagination" is the *name* of the transcendental problem, or is used as a convenient blanket to cover it up. Kant *had* to invent the idea.'[18] It is Nietzsche without the sharp mockery, for Murdoch adds kindly: 'At least, one might add, it stirs thought to advance in the right direction' (Murdoch 1993: 310, emphasis in original).

In order to perceive this unconscious form of imagination through a more conscious one, Murdoch turns to the aesthetic imagination. Whereas the empirical imagination is restricted to automatic performance, as Murdoch understands Kant, the aesthetic imagination is spontaneous and free and able to create a 'second nature' (Murdoch 1992: 314). It may have this freedom, for the aesthetic imagination is limited by Kant to what Murdoch calls the 'small corner' of art. In contrast, Murdoch intends to take the aesthetic imagination out of its corner restricted to art. Her discussion here is occasionally bewildering. Arguments explored in detail elsewhere are omitted here, or succinctly referred to.[19] Murdoch regularly switches between discussing the beautiful, the sublime and genius, without indicating clearly that she is doing so. The present argument consequently relies on these earlier discussions of Kant, in particular 'The Sublime and the Good' and 'The Sublime and the Beautiful Revisited', as the discussion in *Metaphysics as a Guide to Morals* is hard to render on its own.

In these earlier texts even more than in *Metaphysics as a Guide to Morals* the importance of literature for Murdoch's philosophical thinking becomes apparent. Thus, in 'The Sublime and the Beautiful Revisited' Murdoch is simultaneously concerned with a philosophical question ('Is the Liberal-democratic theory of personality an adequate one?') and a literary one ('What is characteristic of the greatest literary works of art?') (Murdoch 1997: 261). In 'The Sublime and the Good' it is only partly in jest that she posits her unswerving belief that 'Shakespeare is the greatest of all artists, and let our aesthetic grow to be the philosophical justification of this judgment' (Murdoch 1997: 205). The earlier texts show how Murdoch's appreciation of great art is decided by the artist's imaginative encounter with another individual. This understanding of great art consequently influences her understanding of philosophical thought, and certainly directs her reading of Kant on imagination.

Considering what notion within Kant's aesthetics may present a form of imagination through which to understand the hidden imagination of perception, Murdoch considers in order the beautiful, the sublime and genius. Her discussion of Kant's notion of the beautiful is brief, and proceeds from her appreciation of particular works of art.[20] She introduces Kant's familiar notion of harmony between the imagination and the understanding, which for him determines the beautiful. The aesthetic imagination, as Murdoch puts it in not exactly Kantian language, 'plays or frolics with the understanding without being governed by empirical concepts' (Murdoch 1993: 311).[21] In an ordinary – not an aesthetic – perception of an object, the empirical imagination prepares a perception for the understanding to attach a concept to the perception according to specific rules. In a free judgement of beauty, in contrast, no given concept is attached to the object observed. Such a judgement is independent of any consideration of purpose.

For Kant, Murdoch argues, '[w]hat is truly beautiful is independent of any interest, it is not tainted either by the good, or by any pleasure extraneous to the act of representing to ourselves the object itself' (Murdoch 1997: 207).[22] In 'The Sublime and the Good' Murdoch notes how Kant's understanding of the beautiful develops into the disinterested view of art, held by many of her contemporaries. An object of art in this view is held to be a thing on its own, judged according to its own rules. Murdoch objects strongly to this understanding of art.[23] It soon becomes apparent that even Kant's understanding of the beautiful does not do.

Murdoch compares Kant's understanding of the beautiful to Tolstoy's theory of art. For Tolstoy, as for Murdoch, art and religion are closely connected. Art 'is the communication of a feeling. ... Art proper ... art in the strictest sense, is not the transmission of any feeling, but only of the highest feelings' (Murdoch 1997: 211). Contemplating these 'promising and serious' assertions Murdoch realizes how 'unnervingly frivolous' Kant's views can seem (Murdoch 1997: 211–212). Kant is chided for not taking art seriously enough.

Murdoch proceeds here in a rather unusual way. She already knows – independent of any aesthetics – which works of art are the best, and that Shakespeare is 'the greatest of all artists', and she subsequently judges aesthetics by the works of art it endorses. Thus, Murdoch's disappointment in Kant's understanding of the beautiful is most palpable when she notes that for Kant the beautiful is restricted to flowers and wallpaper patterns. In *Metaphysics as a Guide to Morals* Murdoch adds in brackets: '(Kant evidently liked flowers, especially tulips.)' (Murdoch 1993: 311). Kant's works of art, Murdoch maintains, aim to be insignificant: 'Kant prefers birdsong to opera. Kant thinks that art is essentially play. Now Shakespeare is great art, and Shakespeare is not play, so Kant must be wrong' (Murdoch 1997: 211).[24] One would hope she is partly in jest. Yet, the limited understanding of what art is and the strict separation of art from anything else in Kant's understanding of the beautiful make Murdoch move swiftly on to the sublime.

In both 'The Sublime and the Good' and in *Metaphysics as a Guide to Morals*, Murdoch explains the sublime in contrasting it with the beautiful. The sublime, other than the beautiful, is connected with emotion. It is strictly said not of objects, but rather of the state of mind that certain objects occasion. The object Kant selects is well known, and Murdoch enumerates 'the overpowering magnitude of a mountain range, the starry sky, the stormy sea, a great waterfall' (Murdoch 1997: 208).

Murdoch alters Kant's understanding of the sublime in two ways. First, for Kant the experience of the sublime results from a conflict between imagination and reason. In the Alps, the imagination fails to satisfy reason's demands. It cannot encompass the magnitude of what is perceived, and thus it cannot satisfy reason's requirements. This failure occasions not just an experience of distress, but also one of exhilaration, as reason's absolute demands are realized.[25] For Murdoch, in contrast, this experience of the failure of the imagination is not redeemed by any hope of grasping the whole (Murdoch 1997: 263). She holds that 'there is no prefabricated harmony, and others are, to an extent we never cease discovering, different from ourselves' (Murdoch 1997: 216).

Second, wondering that '[w]ith the theory of the sublime we have the distressing feeling of some vast and wonderful idea being attached to a trivial occasion' she reconsiders what occasions sublime feelings (Murdoch 1997: 264). Murdoch does not connect the experience of the sublime, and of the limitations of imagination, to the starry heavens. She does not urge us to strain our neck, but rather to look around. The sublime for Murdoch is what may accompany perceiving other people. A true experience of their otherness may occasion a failure of the imagination. Individuals transcend any image formed by the imagination. For Murdoch this failure is – again – not technical but moral. An experience of the sublime reveals the fantastic in the imagination.

Murdoch thus considerably transforms Kant's understanding of imagination, and consequently that of knowledge. Her reading of Kant's aesthetics steadily introduces appraisal in moral terms. In the text under consideration it is only implied that the automatic function of the imagination, which for Kant is an ordinary use of imagination and a crucial part of his theory of understanding, becomes for Murdoch fantasy, or the bad form of imagination. Later on, she will compare it to what Plato considers to be imagination's lower form (Murdoch 1993: 320). The failure of imagination is a much more common event for Murdoch than it is in Kant's epistemology. Any perception of another person that encompasses the person is at odds with her understanding of human beings as endlessly different (Murdoch 1993: 320). Yet, Murdoch still needs a higher form of imagination against the 'automatic' lower form of imagination. She thus proceeds to the notion of genius. Her discussion of genius concludes the discussion of Kant in *Metaphysics as a Guide to Morals*.

Genius is the same as 'superior' imagination. As its main characteristic Murdoch distinguishes its ability to create its own rules. Genius as a form of superior imagination is not decided by general rules (Murdoch 1993: 313).[26] Nor is it possible to explain the rules that are applied in the creation of each unique object, or imitate what a genius creates.[27] This notion of genius allows Murdoch to amend the empirical imagination, and to free it from the law of association. Kant allows the imagination of a genius to be free from this law of association. Yet, the freedom of the genius is strictly confined to the small corner of fine art. Murdoch quotes Kant as saying that 'the imagination (as a *productive* faculty of cognition) is a powerful agent for creating, as it were, *a second nature* out of the material supplied to it by actual nature', but then admits to taking the idea further than its author would have intended (Murdoch 1993: 314; the italics are Murdoch's not Kant's).[28] By taking genius out of the small corner of fine art, Murdoch argues that the world around is constantly being re-created, not by reason, but by imagination (Murdoch 1993: 314). It is not just the rare genius who creates a second nature. Quite the reverse, everyone's imagination constantly makes the world, or makes it up. Murdoch concludes: 'Perception itself is a mode of evaluation.' This conclusion returns throughout the chapter (Murdoch 1993: 315, 328, 329, 334). Art is crucial in understanding ourselves: 'We have to "talk" and our talk will be largely "imaginative" (we are all artists)' (Murdoch 1993: 315).

At this point, the image of the barrier returns:

> The point is, to put it picturesquely, that the 'transcendental barrier' is a huge wide various band (it resembles a transformer such as the lungs in being rather like a sponge) largely penetrable by the creative minds of individuals (though of course we are culturally marked 'children of our time' etc.) and this creativity is the place where the concept of imagination must be placed and defined. (Murdoch 1993: 315)

It is with this image that Murdoch concludes the discussion of imagination in Kant. The formerly impenetrable barrier has become 'a huge wide various band'. The 'automatic' imagination that is essential in the process of understanding is no longer fully separated from the creative imagination with which people make great works of art or tell each other what their day was like. For Murdoch creative imagination may be found in all human activities, from ordinary perception to the most elaborate work of art, from doing the dishes to doing philosophy. The superior kind of imagination is free and creates new objects all the time. Yet, even this kind of imagination is bound to fail when confronted with other people.

What I have assembled here, as a step-by-step reading of the first few pages of chapter eleven of *Metaphysics as a Guide to Morals* on imagination, does not appear as such in the work itself. I have been arguing that Murdoch changes Kant's theory of knowledge. The considerable change is not noted as such by Murdoch. She does not comment on the disappearance of most of Kant's epistemological structures, but rather considers him 'marvellously near the mark'. However, even the rewritten Kant does not supply a full understanding of imagination and fantasy. Thus, Murdoch turns next to Plato.

Plato: the Artist and the Good

If Murdoch's regard for genius has suggested unconditional appreciation for art and artists, her reading of Plato will remove that suggestion instantly. Murdoch considers Plato to be a philosopher who – not unlike herself – is an artist, and yet expresses deep distrust of artists; who supplies his dialogues with persuasive images and yet is wary of imagery for its misleading nature. The distrust of artists, of their imagery, and of imagination Murdoch considers to have been lost in the Romantic understanding of imagination: 'The modern self-conscious concept of "imagination" as something generally exalted is Romantic' (Murdoch 1993: 316).[29] Murdoch clearly distinguishes herself from this modern self-conscious notion of imagination. The Romantic exalted notion may still inspire the recent growing interest in imagination – where some confess the desire to write an unconditional 'Praise of the Imagination' (Brann 1991: 4) – such a notion certainly is not Murdoch's.[30]

So, Kant and Plato both receive much attention in this discussion of imagination, but the Romantics only appear as a brief transition from one to the other. This modest role is exceptional. The Romantic understanding of imagination is generally considered as essential for the contemporary understanding of imagination. Murdoch admits as much in her remark on the modern self-conscious concept of imagination, quoted above. And indeed, for Kearney it introduces the existentialist imagination (Kearney 1988: 181–188). Warnock, in her introduction, half-heartedly admits that '[f]or a long time, and very vaguely ... I believed that Coleridge possessed the secret of the kind of understanding that I sought'. However, she adds: 'Alas, I have given up this faith' (Warnock 1976: 10). Even Murdoch's understanding of imagination is not entirely dissimilar to the Romantic understanding. At least in general terms Murdoch agrees with Romantic authors such as Coleridge or Wordsworth on, for example, the importance of artists for divine or religious revelation and in understanding human beings as first and foremost imaginative.[31]

Yet, throughout her work Murdoch has been invariably critical of ideas she deems Romantic. She admits to appreciating the Romantic Movement for its evaluation of art over science, yet she opposes its 'deification' of art (Murdoch 1993: 85).[32] Murdoch admits that her criticism does not apply to 'the great Romantic artists and thinkers at their best', but to 'the general beaten track' (Murdoch 1997: 368).[33] Romanticism then stands for different ideas descended from the 'great Romantic artists'. This distinction is important. Murdoch does not want to be lured into a discussion on the correct interpretation of 'the great Romantic artists and thinkers at their best'. Her concern is with contemporary ideas.

Most persistent of these is the image of the Romantic man as a lonely man and Romantic art as a self-contained myth (see Murdoch 1997: 264, 266, 279ff., and also 272, respectively).[34] This image of the lonely man is found as early as *Sartre: Romantic Rationalist*. In this first book of philosophy, with its – in this context – telling title, Murdoch calls Sartre a Romantic for embracing a hopeless situation in which one is either to be overcome by a sticky reality or to seize control and establish one's total freedom from everything else.[35] Romantic ideas are still prevalent in contemporary thought and need to be countered in a return to what Murdoch in 'Against Dryness' describes as reality and real human beings: 'We need to turn our attention away from the consoling dream necessity of Romanticism, away from the dry symbol, the bogus individual, the false whole, towards the real impenetrable human person' (Murdoch 1997: 294).

Given these earlier texts it is not surprising that *Metaphysics as a Guide to Morals* provides only a short discussion of the Romantic notion of imagination, and even this is a later addition to the text (cf. Murdoch 1986: 86). Murdoch mentions Coleridge as the one to introduce Kant's notion of imagination in England, but she is reluctant to discuss his work:

> For 'the shaping spirit of imagination' (Coleridge's *Ode to Dejection*) we in England have to wait for what Coleridge learnt from Kant's German successors. Into this morass or dark forest I do not propose to enter but will follow Virgil's advice to Dante, *non ragionem di lor, ma guarda e passa*. (Don't let's talk about them, just look and pass by.) (Murdoch 1997: 316–317)

Just look and pass by. Romantics are here compared to the suffering souls outside the gates of hell, to 'the worthless crew that is hateful to God and to his Enemies' (*Inferno*, III.52). This is a curious comparison, and it is only possible to guess at its rationale. Whether Murdoch considers the Romantics really as worthless as that, one can only speculate, for she follows Virgil's advice.[36] Murdoch 'looks and passes by' the Romantics when considering imagination. She moves on to Plato.

In Plato Murdoch finds a notion of imagination that is not 'exalted'. Her discussion of Plato opens by arguing that he is, in contrast to the Romantics, wary of art and artists, as well as of their imagination. They are in a state of 'eikasia' or 'phantasia', the gloomy situation of the prisoners in the cave, who mistake the shadows of the fire for reality.[37] The state of these prisoners as well as of artists is one of illusion.

Plato is famously remembered for banishing the artists. In *The Republic* they are politely though relentlessly escorted to the borders of the state, if they do not accept a strictly confined role, confined, that is, by the philosopher-rulers. Only puppets are allowed to stay to express the truths of the ideal state (Plato, *The Republic*, 398ab). Plato is alarmed by artists' inability to explain or understand what they are doing. This inability he considers a moral failure. Plato, Murdoch writes, 'connects egoistic fantasy and lack of moral sense with an inability to reflect'.[38] He fears art's ability to charm, which may seduce away from reality by providing easy pleasure.

Yet, for Murdoch this image from *The Republic* does not fully reveal Plato's attitude to artists. Plato for Murdoch always remains both artist and philosopher, and never loses his interest in art. This mixture of art and philosophy is what characterizes the writings of both, as Bronzwaer argues:

> And since Plato was an artist (he set out as a poet and in Iris Murdoch's view no less than in D.H. Lawrence's always remained one), art played a crucial role in his own thinking and is therefore bound to play one in Iris Murdoch's writings, which are in terms of Plato and which are the writings of an artist. (Bronzwaer 1988: 55)

Murdoch notes that Plato does not always treat artists in a hostile way. He allows them, in particular in the earlier dialogues, the gift of divine inspiration, and he does not always disapprove of their inability to explain these gifts (Murdoch 1997: 387).[39] Moreover, Murdoch points out that Plato uses myth, imagery and metaphors in philosophical discussion: 'the artist (or is it the philosopher?) in him still urges to explain by using images' (Murdoch 1997: 445).

Art and philosophy are intertwined in Plato's work, according to Murdoch, and what Plato objects to in art, is not confined to art. Artists are not the only ones to betray 'egoistic fantasy and lack of moral sense'. Instead, Plato's criticism of art stems from a deep mistrust of human nature and of its tendency to look for comfort rather than truth. Humans prefer illusion to reality. In Chapter 1 it was argued how this fallen state of mankind is a persistent theme in Murdoch's thought. She recognizes it in Weil's notion of gravity and argues that Freud 'had provided us with what might be called a doctrine of original sin'. The most eloquent and admittedly 'depressing description' is found in the beginning of 'The Sovereignty of Good Over Other Concepts'.[40]

Not merely artists but everyone can thus be understood to be like a pris-
oner in the cave. Given this image of human beings, morality is for Plato and
for Murdoch not only a matter of acting well from time to time. Though
morality may be expressed in such moments, it is not limited to these. Plato
and Murdoch maintain an image of moral progress or pilgrimage. Humans
are in a state of illusion from which it is not easy to escape. The attempt to do
so is a constant struggle. The intricate attitude of Plato to artists arises from
the fact that in this pilgrimage imagery is necessarily deluding, and yet unavoidable, as Murdoch argues:

> Moral improvement, as we learn from the *Republic*, involves a progressive
> destruction of false images. Image-making or image-apprehending is
> always an imperfect activity, some images are higher than others, that is
> nearer to reality. Images should not be resting places, but pointers
> towards higher truth. The implication is that the highest activities of the
> mind, as in mathematics and mysticism, are imageless. (Murdoch
> 1993: 317–318)

The highest activities of the mind then do not use images, though Murdoch
expresses reservation about considering mathematics as the highest activity of the mind. She claims that Plato does not regard mathematics
as the summit of knowledge and adds that '[t]he Greeks were impressed
and inspired by their own rapid progress in mathematics, especially geome-
try, and likely to see this as an exemplar of understanding' (Murdoch
1993: 318).
Mysticism, in contrast, Murdoch holds in high esteem. Mysticism, both
eastern and western, maintains for Murdoch that 'theological mythology,
stories about gods, creation myths and so on' are at 'a lower level than reality and ultimate religious truth ... beyond the last image we fall into the
abyss of God'. This image she receives from St John of the Cross (Murdoch
1993: 318).[41] Murdoch emphasizes that 'Plato's moral philosophy is *about*
demythologisation'. Indeed, she concludes – albeit with an image – to the
end of all imagery. Images should be regarded 'as ladders, to be thrown
away after use'.
Images pleading for the end of all imagery. Even though Plato and
Murdoch argue that the highest activities of the mind are imageless, to
make this argument imagery is indispensable. While they emphasize and
fear imagery's limitations, they also acknowledge its significance. Their
understanding of imagination is not 'exalted'. Good imagination – as
opposed to bad fantasy – is not solely decided by an artist's consciousness, but as in the myth of the cave it is directed at realities surrounding

the artist and finally at the Good. Good imagery shows itself to be merely that: imagery and not reality.

Murdoch and Plato do not respond identically to the peculiar situation in which imagery is indispensable and yet mistrusted. The divergence in their positions is best explained by pointing out the more political nature of Plato's philosophy. Plato as a politician has a 'strain of unbalance, of violence, of the beginnings of totalitarianism, of unlimitedness. Perhaps also of fear', which Bronzwaer argues Murdoch pictures so well in the young Plato in *Acastos* (Bronzwaer 1988: 63). As a totalitarian politician he distrusts art. 'Art is feared by tyrants', as Murdoch remarks in another context (Murdoch 1993: 90). Thus the artists are politely escorted to the border.

Yet, the puppets are allowed to remain, for Plato also recognizes the necessity of imagery. He has use for imagery for all who cannot manage the deeper understanding of philosophy. While Murdoch expresses her trust in the virtuous peasant to know, and 'to go on knowing, in spite of the removal or modification of the theological apparatus', Plato's Socrates retains artists — albeit the minor ones — for the ideal state. Even the philosophers are given a comparison between the sun and the Good, as well as the allegory of the cave, but above all they must have been charmed by their election as the only ones who can do without imagery. In the creation of this final imagery one might discern a role for the great artist after all. For who would be able to create this imagery, but a philosopher who is also an artist?

It was argued before that for Murdoch — in contrast to Plato — great art in particular can not only play a role in moral progress, but is even considered more important than philosophy. Murdoch does not mind the artists' lack of explanation. In her moral philosophy she denies that 'the unexamined life is not worth living', against the grain of contemporary philosophy (Murdoch 1997: 300). Moral agents and artists are allowed their inability to express the truth or goodness of their work and doings.

In *Metaphysics as a Guide to Morals* Murdoch discerns this capacity of art, thus to play a role in the moral pilgrimage, in what she calls Plato's concept of high imagination. This high imagination, Murdoch holds, is 'passionately creative ... Plato, teaching by images and myths, also acknowledges high imagination as creative stirring spirit, attempting to express and embody what is perfectly good, but extremely remote'. And, Murdoch notes, this 'picture ... implicitly allows a redemption of art' (Murdoch 1993: 319, 320). Thus Murdoch discerns in Plato's understanding of high imagination a possibility to attribute to art this important role in becoming morally better. High imagination looks at a better reality, or even at the Good, when creating. This is, Murdoch argues, what Plato's image of God creating the world expresses.[42]

With this imagery, at the end of this discussion of Plato Murdoch returns to Kant and concludes:

> So it appears that Plato, like Kant, offers two views of imagination. For Plato the lower level, which for Kant is necessary automatic synthesis, is seen in human terms as the production of base illusions, or perhaps simply of the ordinary unimaginative egoistic screen of our conceptualising. . . . The spiritual life is a long disciplined destruction of false images and false goods until (in some sense which we cannot understand) the imagining mind achieves an end of images and shadows. (Murdoch 1993: 320)

In *Metaphysics as a Guide to Morals*, this quotation precedes the distinction between imagination and fantasy with which I started this chapter. *Metaphysics as a Guide to Morals* shows how Murdoch's distinction between imagination and fantasy is based on an idiosyncratic discussion of Kant and Plato. Murdoch's reading of Kant's empirical and aesthetic imagination introduces the ubiquity of imagination, in all perception and thinking. This imagination is not hidden behind any 'unconscious or transcendental barrier', but can be shaped and is best shaped by the imagination of a genius. In the analysis of Plato and his understanding of artists, imagination is further developed as a notion related to reality, and finally to the Good. The Good appears here as both the distant goal at which imagination should be directed and the source of inspiration for high imagination.

Conclusion

The distinction between fantasy and imagination is a defining characteristic of Murdoch's understanding of these notions. The distinction is moral: fantasy is bad and imagination is good. Fantasy denotes an obsession with the self. Imagination denotes attention to reality. The distinction is presented as, in a way, obvious. Just looking at the work of Velasquez or reading Tolstoy can lead to comprehension. However, Murdoch admits too that the distinction may not be clearly distinguished in an artist's or in anyone's mind.

In *Metaphysics as a Guide to Morals* the distinction between fantasy and imagination appears after reflection upon two thinkers: Kant and Plato. In Murdoch's reading of Kant the image of the barrier reveals her understanding of imagination. The crucial step in her reading of his work is releasing the aesthetic imagination out of the limited corner it was allotted by Kant. For Murdoch this notion of imagination also determines the empirical imagination, which is present in all perception. The empirical imagination is not hidden behind a barrier, but behind a threshold. Thus, conscious imagination determines the unconscious imagination to a certain extent. At its best, imagination resembles the creative force of a genius, not following rules but creating a new object. Yet, even this superior kind of imagination is bound to fail when confronted with the reality of others.

Imagination for Murdoch is not fully decided by the individual (artistic) consciousness. In turning to Plato Murdoch reveals not only admiration but also distrust of artists and their imagination. This distrust is an expression of a general distrust of all human beings. Against natural egoistic tendencies Murdoch's reading of Plato posits the importance of reality and ultimately the notion of Good, to which imagination should be directed. Moral pilgrimage is understood as a long destruction of imagery.

The pervasiveness of imagination, discerned in this chapter, reinforces the importance attributed to imagery in the previous chapter. The reading of imagery, inspired by the work of Le Doeuff, is now even more justified by Murdoch's reading of Plato where it turned out to be impossible to philosophize without resort to imagery. This chapter on imagination thus also supports and explains the previous interest in imagery.

Morality, Religion and the Ontological Proof

Introduction

The Good is central to Murdoch's philosophy, as most commentators acknowledge, and it is certainly central to her understanding of imagination and fantasy. For Murdoch the imagination of an artist is not in any way 'exalted'. Instead, it is directed at an independent reality, and ultimately at the Good.

This chapter examines whether it is possible to know the Good, and whether and how it can be argued to exist. The questions are all the more important because for Murdoch little can be learnt from people generally regarded as good: 'Goodness appears to be both rare and hard to picture. It is perhaps most convincingly met with in simple people – inarticulate, unselfish mothers of large families – but these cases are also the least illuminating' (Murdoch 1997: 342).[1] As good people are hard to picture, any answer to the questions 'What is a good man like? How can we make ourselves morally better?' comes in an understanding of the Good rather than in the image of any good person.

In considering the Good, as both direction and source for imagination, this chapter thus returns to questions considered central to Murdoch's work, as well as to the phenomenon that for Murdoch made these questions important: the collapse of religion. The Good can also be understood to explain further Murdoch's notion of reality. The third chapter argued that Murdoch's notion of reality in her earlier writing was up to a certain extent decided by her understanding of literature. The good man who knows 'certain things' about the people around him is like an author in relation to his characters. In later writings, moral goodness is explained in terms of imagination and fantasy, and Murdoch's language becomes more Platonic. The importance of reality in moral progress is complemented by the importance of the Good. To know reality is, in Murdoch's phrasing, to see the world in the light of the Good.

For Murdoch the ontological proof is a most important tool for determining whether the Good exists. The larger part of this chapter considers this proof, as well as the position of the fool to whom it is directed. The most famous conception of this proof one finds in Anselm's *Proslogion*. The proof has had a long and diverse reception. It has been considered as a decisive logical proof for the existence of God, as an assertion of faith or as a self-fulfilling prophecy (cf. Murdoch 1997: 351). Murdoch cites the ontological proof both in her fictional and in her philosophical work.

A discussion of religion precedes that of the ontological proof. For Murdoch the proof is about the Good, not God. In the Good Murdoch intends to preserve what she considers universal and timeless in religion, and of which she regards Christianity as only one expression. In order to understand the ontological proof, it is necessary to examine further Murdoch's understanding of religion. This chapter thus begins with a discussion of the different views on religion expressed in Murdoch's Platonic dialogue 'Above the Gods', one of two dialogues presented in *Acastos* (1986).

'Above the Gods': Morality and Religion

The demise of Christianity is a constant presumption in Murdoch's work, though she avoids the morbid language of the death of God, and rather speaks of the collapse of religion (Murdoch 1997: 337). Even though Murdoch at times admits that her assumption that ' "there is no God" and that the influence of religion is waning rapidly' may be challenged, these challenges are only noted, and never pursued (Murdoch 1997: 361). For Murdoch the present time is that of an 'interregnum' (Murdoch 1966: 101), a time of the angels. The disappearance of God has unleashed messengers, but it is impossible to know whose message they bring. Murdoch's characters constantly live and discuss this interregnum, sometimes to their own fairly honourable defeat, and at other times quite comfortably between treacle tart and coffee (Murdoch 1966: 97–103).

A revealing discussion on religion is also found in one of Murdoch's Platonic dialogues in *Acastos*: 'Above the Gods: A Dialogue about Religion' (first published in 1980). The discussion between the different characters expresses the particular angle from which Murdoch regards religion. The dialogue's significance lies both in the ideas considered in this discussion and in the ones ignored. It focuses on the notion of Good, and possible differences between morality and religion, but disregards for instance a sense of community, or any interest in sacred texts.[2] *Acastos* has been ignored by some commentators and severely criticized by others. Nussbaum's review concludes that the dialogues are 'not Platonic dialogues. Their failure of thought is a failure of imagination' (Nussbaum 1986a: 881). While I would

agree with Nussbaum's conclusion, and even most of her criticism, I nevertheless hold that 'Above the Gods' provides essential introduction to Murdoch's thoughts on religion and to her understanding of the ontological
proof. 'Above the Gods' shows the limitations of Murdoch's thoughts on
religion, yet these are limitations that Murdoch would be the first to
acknowledge. It is where Murdoch starts making jokes.[3]

The topic of discussion has come up at the characters' return from a religious festival, and they go back at the end. The festival provides the oppor-
tunity to start discussing religion. The beginning also duplicates the opening
of *The Republic*, and as such may be understood as homage to Plato. Yet, no
philosopher-king emerges from 'Above the Gods'. The dialogue's central
interest is not a political one. So, even if the beginning has been interjected
as a reminder that new communities, in particular religious communities,
have often originated at festivals of the established religions, Murdoch does
not pursue the political implications.

The established religion is of little importance to the dialogue. The characters all attend the festival, yet most of them, with the exception of the servant and perhaps Socrates, don't believe in the gods who are honoured.[4]
Belief in the gods is considered to be something of the past, and the garlands
infected with fleas reveal the deplorable state of religion: the garlands are
worn while the flowers look nice, but quickly discarded when fleas are dis-
covered (Murdoch 1997: 497–498; cf. 507). And thus, they discuss religion,
but none of them really confesses to being a religious man.

The description of religion, as belief in God or in gods, remains, moreover,
sufficiently vague to apply to both Greek mythology and Christianity. Even
though these Greek men as citizens of ancient Athens talk about the gods in
the plural, the gods remain without any qualification and the men might as
well have been talking about the one God of Christianity. It is indeed most
likely that they are.[5] God is here the God of philosophers, the God who
received his name from Pascal's famous testament, and the conversation is
consequently that of philosophers of religion.[6] God or the gods represent an
idea to which general concepts are attributed. These men do not consider
gods known from religious experience, or from any particular religious practice or text. Their God is primarily a structuring principle in politics or morality and their main concern is the question of what may replace God's
usefulness in this context.[7]

Even when Murdoch lets Acastos take issue with a contemporary
issue in the Anglican Church – in only the slightest of disguises – her arguments are not concerned with belief, or the actual practice of that religion.
Acastos comments: 'when the priests change the old-fashioned language
into modern words it sounds so ugly and awkward, it loses spiritual force'

(Murdoch 1997: 507). This clearly echoes Murdoch's complaint that the 'loss of lively and natural access to the Authorised Version of the Bible and Cranmer's Book of Common Prayer is a literary loss comparable to losing touch with Shakespeare. It is also, whether or not one believes in God, a spiritual loss' (Murdoch 1979: 5). The loss is first called literary, and second spiritual, but even then it does not matter whether one believes in God or not. Particular belief is not the issue here.

Socrates may suggest that '[q]uite a lot of educated people believe in gods', but the others are not persuaded. Belief is left to the servant. This should not be taken to suggest that for Murdoch only the uneducated can be religious. Rather, Murdoch's principal interest does not lie with religious people, but with those people whom she calls in 'On "God" and "Good"' 'unreligious believers'. Her work is about and for these people. They can no longer imagine any return to the previous belief, but at the same time regret the loss of religion for different reasons. In this time of angels Murdoch endeavours to retain what she deems to be religion's essentials.[8]

In the absence of any professed belief in God the discussion promptly shifts to morality. Religion is only considered for its moral dimension. Or, one may argue, the term religion is used to emphasize the serious nature of morality, as an angry young Plato declares in 'Above the Gods': 'Anyhow, morality, if it's anything serious, is something religious' (Murdoch 1997: 514). Similarly, in *Metaphysics as a Guide to Morals*, Murdoch maintains that religion may be called moral philosophy 'so long as it treats those matters of "ultimate concern", our experience of the unconditioned and our continued sense of what is holy' (Murdoch 1993: 511–12; cf. Schweiker 1996: 209).[9] It is doubtful, however, whether this use of the term is generally recognizable. *Acastos'* Plato later confesses not to have much use for the notion of religion, precisely because 'people think of religion as something exotic and formal, and a bit aside from life, whereas what I mean is everywhere, like breathing' (Murdoch 1997: 519).

This discussion of religion is thus limited in various ways: it is not explicitly concerned with one religion in particular, and none of the speakers is a believer. The main concern is to find a proper substitute for the gods in the moral lives of unreligious believers. Yet, this serious topic is constantly undermined by the form of the text. It has been noted before that the dialogue structure is prevalent within Murdoch's thinking. It presents itself not only in *Acastos*, but also in *Metaphysics as a Guide to Morals*.[10] Yet, *Acastos* more explicitly reveals this form and thus more naturally invites consideration of this form. In favouring the dialogue form Murdoch again expresses her admiration for Plato. Like Plato she considers it impossible to state philosophy's ultimate concerns. In *The Fire and the Sun* she refers to Plato's *Seventh Letter* especially in support of this statement: 'The *Seventh Letter* makes the same point even more emphatically. What is really important in philosophy cannot be put into written words and scarcely indeed into words. (Language itself may be a barrier)' (Murdoch 1997: 405). A dialogue, with its unfinished, interrupted thoughts, and undermining banter, exposes the limitations of the thoughts and arguments developed. It thus inhibits a reading in which one position is considered as ultimate truth.[11] The limitations of language are most pressing where the notion of the Good is concerned.[12]

In this dialogue about religion, the characters' minds are not exclusively occupied by this topic. The discussion is larded with their expressions of love, sexual desire or jealousy for one another. This sexual play both invigorates and undermines the discussion. In their love for Socrates his friends try to stretch their minds while at the same time ridiculing each other's ideas. In particular the entrance of Alcibiades at the end of the dialogue and his constant mockery of Plato undermine the discussion as a whole. Alcibiades enters the discussion just after Socrates has confessed to liking Plato's words and to loving him while he speaks. Plato reveals great anxiety by asking if he is not loved all the time. At this delicate moment Alcibiades bursts in, establishing himself immediately as a serious rival:

SOCRATES: Plato has been telling us about being in love.
ALCIBIADES: My subject too!
TIMONAX: He's in love with Good.
ALCIBIADES: Is it mutual? (Murdoch 1997: 522)

In a typically Murdochian iconoclastic move the reader is left feeling uncertain about the worth of anything said before.

As is often the case with banter, Alcibiades' remark is not only comic, but also touches upon a serious difficulty in Murdoch's understanding of the Good. The question, whether the Good is as much in love with Plato as Plato is with the Good, recalls of 'someone's' objection in 'On "God" and "Good"' that it

makes sense to speak of loving God, a person, but very little sense to speak of loving Good, a concept. 'Good' even as a fiction is not likely to inspire, or even be comprehensible to, more than a small number of mystically minded people who, being reluctant to surrender 'God', fake up 'Good' in his image, so as to preserve some kind of hope. The picture is not only purely imaginary, it is not even likely to be effective.

And, the objector continues, would it not be better to give up all metaphysical speculation, now that the concept of God the father is 'outdated' and 'rely on simple popular utilitarianism and existentialist ideas, together with a little empirical psychology, and perhaps some doctored Marxism, to keep the human race going'? Murdoch immediately admits to be 'often more than half persuaded to think in these terms' (Murdoch 1997: 358–9). Likewise, in 'Above the Gods' Alcibiades wonders whether Plato's Good is not purely imaginary, thought up by a poetic mind. Did he not on entering ask Plato whether he had 'written any poems lately, dear? Love poems?' (Murdoch 1997: 521).

Murdoch makes all the characters in the dialogue present what she understands to be a prominent view on religion. The first two speakers consider religion from a political perspective. Antagoras is characterized as 'a sophist, in love with Timonax', who is identified as 'a socially conscious youth'. Next are Acastos, 'a serious questioning youth' and a servant. They present an argument from the obvious, as the virtuous peasant and his more educated counterpart. The dialogue culminates when Socrates questions a young and angry Plato. They are interrupted by Alcibiades, who enters near the end of the dialogue (Murdoch 1997: 496 and 521 respectively).[13] In the speeches of Plato, Alcibiades and Socrates Murdoch discusses her most personal and pressing ideas.

Antagoras finds only one use for religion, which is to control the uneducated masses, to which he considers himself (intellectually and morally) superior: 'So long as there's an uneducated mob, there's a place for something like religion' (Murdoch 1997: 501). He emphasizes the use of fear religion may instil. His position is – perhaps not surprisingly – based on the contested distinction between fact and value – to which Murdoch draws our attention by means of italics – which for him ensues from 'independent moral men making up their minds and choosing their values' (Murdoch 1997: 500).

Antagoras' conclusion infuriates young Timonax. Timonax is young and a fiery communist (*avant-la-lettre*). His characterization of religion as 'a drug to stop people from resisting tyranny' (Murdoch 1997: 503) recalls of course Marx' 'opium of the people'. Unlike Antagoras, whom he accuses of cynicism and elitism, Timonax has much confidence in the masses (Murdoch 1997: 501). He trusts that equality and brotherhood, and morality as something 'absolute', as *'caring about people'*, would be possible, if it were not for religion (Murdoch 1997: 504). Yet, his outburst, vehement as it may be, is not given much reflection. Socrates is quick to point out an inaccuracy in Timonax' reasoning, but more devastatingly, he confesses that Timonax' eloquence makes him tired. Antagoras merely ridicules him.

These positions of reactionary and communist do not return in the remainder of the dialogue, though Antagoras and Timonax will offer serious though short challenges to the ideas of the others. Murdoch does not entirely disregard the political consequences of thought or her own aspiration to speak for or even control the masses. Perhaps, Timonax represents part of her younger self, and Antagoras her older self, who is both in love and annoyed with his youth. Yet, politics is not her primary concern when considering religion. Antagoras and Timonax state their positions, but these are not much explored.

When Socrates starts questioning the next person, young and serious Acastos, the dialogue changes direction. The questions Socrates asks shift from equating religion with belief in God or gods to distinguishing religion from morality.[14] He also changes his role from questioning to more positively stating what he deems to be the case. Unlike Antagoras and Timonax, Acastos is not stating positive theories, but rather stuttering his answers. Acastos is a nice and perhaps even a good person. He notices 'certain things' around him. His concern for fleas recalls James in *The Sea, The Sea*.[15] Unlike Antagoras and Timonax he does not regard the slave as an object, though he does not feel comfortable in talking to him. He is also friendly to Plato, offering him a seat at the beginning and taking him along to the festival at the end.

Acastos talks very much with the sort of emphasis that is characteristic for many of the discussions in Murdoch's novels, and which gives them their unique and also peculiar timbre. One can only speculate about the use of this idiosyncratic device. I would suggest that it attempts to convey a sense of knowing something for sure while at the same time being at a loss to express what is known with so much certainty. It is, of course, also open to easy ridicule.

ACASTOS: I think religion *contains* morality. It goes beyond common sense, it goes beyond that sort of limited attitude, dividing the world into manageable bits. Religion is believing that your life is a *whole* − I mean that goodness and duty are just *everywhere* − like *always* looking further and deeper − and feeling *reverence* for things − a religious person would care about everything in that sort of way, he'd feel everything mattered and every second mattered. (Murdoch 1997: 508)

His ideas and metaphors remind one of Murdoch's own words, as in the earlier quotation of his criticism on the change from traditional to modern language. Constantly questioned by Socrates Acastos struggles with the paradox of being 'drawn to the idea of a sort of central − good − something very real' (Murdoch 1997: 506), which at the same time cannot be named. He wonders whether religion can go on existing yet without lying, and does not 'want worship and ritual and prayer and so on just to *go* — there's a valuable — precious — thing somewhere inside it all'. This something is more remembered than invented (Murdoch 1997: 507). Yet, when pressed by Socrates, Acastos is almost moved to tears, crying — in italics — that he doesn't know (Murdoch 1997: 509–510).

The simplicity of the slave, who is next questioned, is of a different nature. The simple truth he embodies and his belief in the gods defy the logic of the debating men. He cannot comprehend that they ask what God is like, or that they ask after the reasons why the gods should be loved. In his broken language he explains to the men what God is like and how he is everywhere and everything for him. Antagoras and Timonax make fun of him, but Acastos is embarrassed. It is interesting to compare this embarrassment to that felt by readers at the presence of this 'embarrassingly caricatured' slave (Nussbaum 1986a: 881). This embarrassment may be partly lifted on consideration that the slave may not primarily convey what Murdoch perceives to be the position of ordinary people. If anything, it is a rhetorical device — as are all the indistinguishable aunties and mothers in Murdoch's philosophical work. As such, this unarticulated, possibly worthwhile, belief is disruptive, and makes not just the position of the others, but their whole conversation uncomfortable.

It is not a coincidence that this disruptive element precedes Plato's speech. One would assume that Plato is Murdoch's spokesperson, just as Socrates is considered to be Plato's. Yet, the theatrical aspects of the dialogue constantly question this interpretation. Plato is unsocial and obsessed with Socrates, as well as indifferent if not hostile to the others. His talk of something absolute is introduced with the undermining sense of comedy so typical of Murdoch's writing:

> SOCRATES: What is this 'it' that you're certain of in this special unique way, which isn't God and which has to exist and is proved by everything and is seen in the clear light beyond the shadows?
> PLATO: Good.
> ANTAGORAS: What did he say?
> PLATO: *Good.* (Murdoch 1997: 514)

Plato's ideas are, especially in comparison with Acastos', notably psychological, in the sense that they have to do with the *psyche*. He distinguishes its different levels: one part is concerned with truth and reality, the rest consists of mere fantasies and 'selfish tricks'. Deeply moral or religious change is compared to learning mathematics or a trade. Thus one may learn that there is something outside us, and so to forget oneself (Murdoch 1997: 515–516). One may even learn this from falling in love. At Socrates' suggestion Plato eagerly admits that there is a god after all and his name is Eros, or rather that Eros is 'a holy passionate spirit . . . *in love* with the Good' (Murdoch 1997: 518). In spite of his sceptical audience Plato maintains that everyone 'instinctively' knows that 'good is real and absolute, not optional and relative, all their life proves it' (Murdoch 1997: 519). Moral philosophy, for Plato as for Acastos, is everywhere.

This obviously Murdochian position, held by the volatile youth Plato, is immediately crushed by the entrance of Alcibiades. Alcibiades is above all an iconoclast. He has, as Antagoras suggests, castrated all the statues of the gods. This literal desecration is preceded by a figurative one, for by being offended by the gods for 'flaunting their organs at us' (his reason for castrating them) Alcibiades has first brought the gods down to the level of ordinary humans. He has made them subject to human morality.

> SOCRATES: I imagine you wouldn't call yourself a religious man?
> ANTAGORAS: Was it you who castrated all those statues of the gods?
> ALCIBIADES: Ssssh! The gods deserve to be castrated. Who are they to flaunt their organs at us? But have you really been talking about *them*? (*pointing upwards*) (Murdoch 1997: 521–2)

In a constant mockery of Plato and his sexual jealousy Alcibiades declares that religion is power: 'evil isn't really evil, good isn't really good, we pass beyond the ordinary childish abstract notions of good and evil, and enter into the unity of the world!' (Murdoch 1997: 523). Plato physically attacks him for his thoughts in a bloodthirsty desire to kill them. Alcibiades is highly amused.

If nothing else this derisive Nietzschean response allows Socrates to turn away from the elaborate arguments to common sense and simplicity.[16] He argues for simply trying to be good and seeing the extent in which religion and morality are allies and the extent in which one should live by external rules: 'Goodness is simple, it's just very difficult' (Murdoch 1997: 525). This plea for simplicity amuses Alcibiades and evokes a solemn reaction from Plato. Even though Socrates has beseeched him not to make a drama of it, Plato decides to kneel at what he perceives to be a newly built shrine.

Socrates' plea for simplicity here is reminiscent of the beginning of 'The Idea of Perfection'. In a reproach to a well-known phrase of the earlier Socrates ('the unexamined life is not worth living'), Murdoch argues that 'it must be possible to do justice to both Socrates and the virtuous peasant'.[17] In 'Above the Gods' Murdoch warns the debating intellectuals not to disregard simple answers, where an intellectual approach is naturally likely to favour an intellectual answer. Yet, Murdoch's Socrates, unlike Plato's Socrates, pleads simplicity. 'Above the Gods' endorses simplicity, through the constant presence of the servant, through persistent warnings against preference for the own (intellectual) approach as well as through wariness of Plato's too violent feelings that the answer cannot be simple. The dialogue ends when the characters return to the festival in order to, as Socrates puts it, 'enjoy our gods while we can'. He walks away, 'affectionately arm in arm with Alcibiades'. Socrates does not mind the latter's ideas, but Plato does. Alcibiades is amused by Socrates' plea for simplicity, but Plato can't bear it. The stage directions instruct the actor to 'hold his bursting head' (Murdoch 1997: 526).

'Above the Gods' has thus introduced the main ideas and difficulties Murdoch encounters when introducing the Good into philosophy. In both 'Above the Gods' and 'On "God" and "Good"' the Good appears after observing the decline of religion. In 'On "God" and "Good"' Murdoch notices a void in philosophy, as it is unable to rescue the values involved in the collapse of religion. The essay attempts to retain in the notion of the Good a central concept with the characteristics of the old God (Murdoch 1997: 344). 'Above the Gods' features a discussion of characters who, inspired by love for one another and in particular for Socrates, consider moral philosophy after religion. Even though religion may not be their prime concern, their (tacit) understanding of religion determines discussion of moral philosophy. Religion is understood as belief in God or gods, yet none of the characters confesses to actually believing, the servant and perhaps Socrates excepted.

'Above the Gods' shows the various limitations in Murdoch's understanding of religion. Theologians may find a rather sparse concept of religion. Political concerns are only side issues. More importantly when focusing on Murdoch's own philosophy it shows the difficulties for understanding the Good. In this dialogue, more than in her philosophical essays, Murdoch is able to question and even mock her own ideas. Is the Good at all useful? Is it anything but the invention of a jealous poet? Murdoch is never able to abandon completely these doubts. The Good may be known instinctively, but how does it stand up in any discussion? 'Above the Gods' thus reveals the positions that alternately decide Murdoch's contemplation of the Good, and the subsequent discussion of the ontological proof: Plato's desire to build shrines, Socrates' plea for simplicity and Alcibiades' iconoclasm, as well as the servant's presence. What argument is able to defend the Good against Alcibiades? The ontological argument? Does it matter that Murdoch disregards many aspects of religion?

The Ontological Proof: The 'Belief' that the Proof Tries to 'Prove'

In particular Murdoch's later oeuvre affirms the importance of the proof for her philosophical thinking. It first occurs in 'On "God" and "Good"'', where Murdoch remarks that 'the ontological proof is seen to be not exactly a proof but rather a clear assertion of faith . . . which could only confidently be made on the basis of a certain amount of experience' (Murdoch 1997: 351; cf. 349). In *The Fire and the Sun* she calls it 'Plato's main idea' (Murdoch 1997: 458). The proof next appeared as the topic of one of her Gifford lectures in 1982. Murdoch used this text again in the Van der Leeuw lecture in Groningen, in 1987, and in 1992, in *Metaphysics as a Guide to Morals*, she devotes two chapters to it. The proof is also interjected by the most mystically minded characters in her novels from *The Unicorn* onwards.[18]

The importance of this proof has been generally recognized. Conradi points out that 'the ontological proof has deep roots in Murdoch's thought' (Conradi 2001a: 392 n. 13). It is discussed by more than half of the contributors to *Iris Murdoch and the Search for Human Goodness*. The proof also has an important place in Antonaccio's *Picturing the Human*. She argues that '[Murdoch's] account of the good is validated by a version of the ontological proof' (Antonaccio 2000: 15).

The present discussion of the ontological proof principally considers Murdoch's reading of Anselm in *Metaphysics as a Guide to Morals*, while also remembering the different characters of 'Above the Gods'. The contrast between the learned and the simple encountered in 'Above the Gods' returns at the end of *Metaphysics as a Guide to Morals*' (first) chapter on the ontological proof when Murdoch writes:

> An ultimate religious 'belief' must be that even if all 'religions' were to blow away like mist, the necessity of virtue and the reality of the good would remain. This is what the Ontological Proof tries to 'prove' in terms of a unique formulation. This is for thinkers to look at. The ordinary fellow 'just knows', for one is speaking of something which is in a sense obvious, the unique nature of morality. (Murdoch 1993: 428)

This quote distinguishes the thinkers from the ordinary fellows. The proof as well as its object − the necessity of virtue and the reality of the Good − is for thinkers to look at. Whoever looks at the proof is identified not as an ordinary fellow who 'just knows' (in quotation marks), but as a thinker who looks at this ultimate religious 'belief' (in quotation marks) that the ontological proof tries to 'prove' (also in quotation marks). Murdoch thus re-creates the environment of 'Above the Gods' where the learned discussed religion in the presence of an ordinary believer. As in the dialogue, the ordinary fellow may be regarded as an object of ridicule or desire, or a cause of embarrassment, but he or she does not really take part in the discussion.

Looking at the proof is, however, a rather complicated matter, witness its many and diverse interpretations. Looking at it does not at all guarantee that the thinker will find what the ordinary fellow 'just knows'. On the contrary, it may obscure and diffuse the 'ultimate religious "belief" ... that even if all "religions" were to blow away like mist, the necessity of virtue and the reality of the good would remain'. For various thinkers have dismissed the proof for convincing reasons. As a way to the 'belief' then the approach of the thinker may not be the most secure one. It may not even be a feasible one. Murdoch's distinction between thinkers and ordinary fellows thus introduces an important point of debate in the reception of this proof. It has been argued that the ontological proof is not so much a proof as an affirmation of faith. If this is the case, it cannot be proven or understood from any (thinker's) faithless position.

This affirmation of faith has, moreover, been said to be personal.[19] Murdoch observes that it is 'a proof which a man can only give to himself, herein resembling *cogito ergo sum*, to which it is indeed related by Descartes' (Murdoch 1993: 392). The ontological proof thus considered is different from any proof of which the outcome may be accepted by testimony. There are many such proofs, which one does not prove oneself, because it suffices to trust someone else's expertise. The ontological proof, on the contrary, has to be proven by each individual.

For Murdoch these two aspects, the importance of faith and of proving the proof individually, set the ontological proof apart from all other proofs, but do not affect its importance:

> Yet these reminders do not set the Proof aside as a piece of history or items of private piety, and in spite of having been apparently demolished by Kant it has continued to interest philosophers and theologians. *Credo ut intelligam* (I believe in order to understand) is not just an apologist's paradox, but an idea with which we are familiar in personal relationships, in art, in theoretical studies. I have faith (important place for this concept) in a person or idea in order to understand him or it, I intuitively know or grasp more than I can yet explain. (Murdoch 1993: 392–3)

In Murdoch's explanation of *credo ut intelligam*, this faith does not belong to a specific person or group. It is not expressed by any particular religious belief, but it is 'an idea with which we are familiar in personal relationships, in art, in theoretical studies'. The faith considered by Murdoch is recognized by all. It is the faith in persons and beliefs that goes beyond explanation.

If this faith is not a specific faith, what about the 'belief' that the ontological proof tries to 'prove'? Anselm, in the most famous formulation of the proof, considers God to be the object of the proof. It has been pointed out that his understanding of God as 'that than which nothing greater can be thought' is not merely Christian. A similar phrase is found in Seneca. However, it is likely that Anselm found the origin of the phrase 'that than which nothing greater can be thought' in a text by one of the church fathers: Augustine's *De libero arbitrio*.[20] In comparison, Murdoch refers to the object of the proof as 'an ultimate religious "belief" . . . that even if all "religions" were to blow away like mist, the necessity of virtue and the reality of the good would remain'. She provides yet another explication by twice quoting Tillich, at the beginning of both chapters on the ontological proof in *Metaphysics as a Guide to Morals*. In this quotation from his *Systematic Theology* Tillich speaks of 'the acknowledgement of the unconditional element in the structure of reason and reality' (Murdoch 1993: 391–392 and 431).[21] These descriptions are not the same. In Murdoch's reading, the proof is no longer considered within a particular religious tradition, but with belief that goes beyond different religious traditions. Again, Murdoch seems to be writing most of all for unreligious believers, and again – just as she did when reading Kant – Murdoch does not consider all of Anselm's concerns, but rather appropriates his ideas in order to answer the question 'How can we make ourselves morally better?'

What then does the proof prove for Murdoch? She hesitates to describe the import of this proof, which is apparent from her abundant use of quotation marks. What kind of belief is one in quotation marks that is proven in quotation marks? How can it be called religious when it is to remain even if all religions in quotation marks were to blow away like mist? To what extent is Murdoch creating or ordering this belief by stating that it *must be*, not that it *is*? An answer to these questions is sought in considering first the object of the proof and then the position of the unbeliever or fool.

The Different Arguments in Anselm's *Proslogion*

Most of the writing on Anselm's *Proslogion* concentrates on only three of its 26 chapters. These three, chapters two, three and four, constitute the famous ontological argument for the existence of God. This argument has fascinated thinkers, even to the extent to which they felt it impossible not to take a stand. Some have tried to formulate its final refutation (Gaunilo, Thomas Aquinas, Gassendi, Kant, Russell), others to find new positive versions of the old argument (Duns Scotus, Descartes, Spinoza, Leibniz, Hegel, Hartshorne).[22]

The fascination principally concerns these three chapters, yet by singling these out one directly enters the discussion on the interpretation of the proof. The inclusion or exclusion of the first chapter is especially significant. This introductory chapter, an 'Exhortation of the mind to the contemplation of God', is a prayer. Anselm laments his inability to find God and his unfortunate fate that has removed him from God's presence. He expresses his desire to see God and he asks for his help.

This prayer is a moving and beautiful piece of prose, yet is it also part of the proof? The answer to this question is decided by the importance one attributes to faith. Those who regard the ontological proof as a rational argument consider this first chapter to be merely literary ornamentation. For those who underline the importance of faith it is more truly introductory. For them the prayer reveals Anselm's intentions and argumentation. In the ontological proof Anselm looks for reasons that will support his belief. The prayer reveals his desire to come thus closer to God as well as his sorrow at his present distance from him.[23] The prayer brings Anselm and his readers into a proper disposition for the proof. It concentrates the mind on the relationship with God.

Murdoch quotes a few lines from this first chapter, which she calls a preface to the proof, in order to argue that possible limitations to the proof – the 'context of deep belief and disciplined spirituality' (Murdoch 1993: 392) – are not real limitations. That the proof is preceded by faith is nothing unusual, but in contrast something 'with which we are familiar . . . Faith (loving belief) and knowledge often have an intimate relation which is not easy to analyse in terms of what is prior to what' (Murdoch 1993: 393). Again, Murdoch moves, with remarkable ease, from a specific faith to a general observation about human psychology. She seems most of all intent on reassuring her audience that Anselm's proof does not proceed from unfamiliar grounds. Even those without any awareness of the Christian faith can understand what it is to 'have faith . . . in a person or idea in order to understand him or it' (Murdoch 1993: 393). At this point in the text Murdoch disregards any difference between having faith in God and having faith in something else.

Murdoch moves swiftly to what she calls the proof's 'first formulation', in *Proslogion*'s chapter II, in which 'God is taken to be the *Ens Realissimum, aliquid quo nihil maius cogitari possit*, the most real being, than which nothing greater [or more perfect] can be conceived' (Murdoch 1993: 393). The Latin quote is not exactly the same as the text in *Proslogion* chapter II. Anselm does not use the term *Ens Realissimum*, the most real being. The

addition of *Ens Realissimum* is remarkable, for it is in disagreement with
both the logical and the transcendental understanding of Anselm's argument, to be discussed shortly. Nevertheless, I doubt if one should attribute much importance to this addition where Murdoch's understanding of
the proof is concerned. Her interest in the proof does not really concern this
first formulation.

After describing God as 'that than which nothing greater can be conceived' Anselm wonders if there is 'no such nature, since the fool hath said
in his heart, there is no God (Psalm XIV.I)' (Anselm 1974: 7). Yet, he
argues, the fool surely understands what he hears and what he understands
is in his understanding. Anselm then reasons that it is greater to exist in the
understanding *and* in reality, than to exist only in the understanding. Thus,
if that than which nothing greater can be conceived only exists in the
understanding it would not be that than which nothing greater can be conceived (Anselm 1974: 8). The crux of this argument is the negative description of God. God is not posited as a positive entity, but as something that is
always greater. For every positive understanding of God, it is possible to
think of something greater. It is thus by indirect demonstration that one
has to conclude to his actual existence. The argument has also been called
a *reductio ad absurdum* of the atheist position. If God only existed in the mind,
he would not be God. Therefore he does not only exist in the mind, but also
in reality.[24]

Murdoch stresses in her reading that this formulation of the proof distinguishes between existing in the mind (*in intellectu*) and existing in reality
(*in re*): 'To exist *in re* is taken to be a quality (predicate), in the case of something good a perfection, which is *extra* to that of existing only *in intellectu*'
(Murdoch 1993: 393). The idea of God, which we, Murdoch writes, can
surely understand, entails his existence. If God did not exist he would lack
a quality (i.e. existence) and not be 'that than which nothing greater can be
conceived'. By using the notions 'quality' and 'predicate' Murdoch calls to
mind the criticism Kant and Russell levelled at the ontological proof. She
points out that they contended that '[t]he idea of existence adds nothing to
a concept, existence is not a predicate'. It does not make sense to call existing
in reality 'greater' than existing in the understanding alone. The notion of
existence is already included in the believer's understanding of God (Murdoch 1993: 394).[25] Couched in these words, it is clear why Murdoch mentions Kant's criticism only briefly. She has acknowledged all along that this
proof proceeds from a position of faith, i.e. from belief in God's existence.
Moreover, Kant's criticism does not affect, for Murdoch, the more important transcendental argument.

Murdoch's attention quickly shifts to the question whether 'we can surely understand' the idea of God. She notes how Gaunilo, who, Murdoch claims, 'of course believed in God', first queried this possibility: ' "I do not know that reality itself which God is, nor can I frame a conjecture of that reality from some other reality. For you yourself assert that there can be nothing else like it" ' (Murdoch 1993: 394, quoting Anselm 1974: 148). And, Gaunilo adds, would it not be possible to argue anything into existence? There are two different objections here. First, it is argued that it is not possible to understand 'that than which nothing greater can be conceived'. Second, the argument need not be confined to God's existence alone. Gaunilo thus famously suggested that the existence of a perfect island may be proven in like manner (Anselm 1974: 150–151).

Murdoch considers the second objection first, moving on to what she regards as a clarification of the first argument. This clarification is found in *Proslogion*'s third chapter and in Anselm's answer to Gaunilo. Here Anselm argues that he is not concerned with God's incidental existence, but with God's unique, necessary existence. God does not exist in the way that other beings exist, for he cannot be thought of as not existing.[26] Murdoch writes: 'The definition of God as having *necessary* not contingent existence is an important clarification for any interested party' (Murdoch 1993: 395). This important clarification moves the argument away from the indirect demonstration, and according to Antonaccio (an interested party), away from its original logical nature, into a transcendental argument proving a necessary structure in consciousness, where Murdoch considers the Good rather than God the object of the ontological proof (Antonaccio 2000: 126).

In *Picturing the Human* Antonaccio comprehensively examines Murdoch's understanding of the ontological proof. In the first chapter she asserts that '[Murdoch's] account of the good is validated by a version of the ontological proof' (Antonaccio 2000: 15). After the extensive discussion in chapter five she maintains in her sixth and final chapter that 'the proof reveals that the good is an objective principle of perfected moral knowledge that is only accessible through the medium of "personal resonance" ', and that 'Murdoch justifies this reflexive argument with a version of the ontological proof' (Antonaccio 2000: 165 and 169 respectively). Antonaccio meticulously examines possible objections to the proof and shows how Murdoch refutes these. Throughout my discussion I shall be returning to Antonaccio's interpretation. As 'validation' and 'justification' it would have pleased young Plato, but it also affects the position of the fool, which I consider later.

When examining the transcendental argument Antonaccio repeatedly argues that the object of the proof is grasped through consciousness.

Murdoch, Antonaccio argues, 'reads Anselm's proof along much the same lines as Charles Taylor. God's existence is grasped as necessarily real in and through the structures of human knowing' (Antonaccio 2000: 126; Taylor 1989: 140).[27] Indeed, in Taylor Antonaccio finds two important points for Murdoch's understanding of the proof: 'the proof takes its starting point in consciousness' and, second, 'according to the proof the idea of God *must* occur to us, because it is the very condition for our consciousness of ourselves as "selves"' (Antonaccio 2000: 124, emphasis in original). The human consciousness while reflecting on 'that than which nothing greater can be conceived' has to acknowledge what both presupposes and surpasses all of its activities.

The transcendental argument thus conceives of God's existence as unique and necessary. The object of the proof, according to Murdoch,

> cannot be a particular, a contingent thing, one thing among others; a contingent god might be a great demonic or angelic spirit, but not the Being in question. . . . God's necessary existence is connected with his not being an object. God is not to be worshipped as an idol or identified with any empirical thing; as is indeed enjoined by the Second Commandment. (Murdoch 1993: 395; cf. Antonaccio 2000: 125–126)

So, the proof takes as its starting-point something that, as it turns out, is unlike all other things. Even to call it some*thing* can be misleading (Antonaccio 2000: 125–126). In order to express the singularity of this situation Murdoch uses different expressions. She remarks that God's '*non-existence is impossible*', that he exists necessarily, that only in this case 'if you can conceive of this entity you are *ipso facto* certain that what you are thinking of is real', that God is not 'one thing among others', and not an object (Murdoch 1993: 395). These different phrases are directed at Gaunilo's second objection, that it would be possible to argue anything into existence.

However, even if these phrases manage to refute the second objection, they reinforce at the same time Gaunilo's first objection that it is not possible to understand 'that than which nothing greater can be conceived', raising the question of the meaning of the notions 'existence', 'reality', 'object' and 'ontological'. In order to remove this first objection, a – what Murdoch calls – *metaphysical* argument is supplied in addition to the *transcendental* argument. Anselm's answer to Gaunilo is, strictly speaking, twofold.[28] Anselm first replies by appealing to Gaunilo's 'faith and conscience to attest that this is most false' (Anselm 1974: 154). Next, he provides an answer that is 'evident to any rational mind', and even to 'the fool who does not accept sacred authority' (Anselm 1974: 167–168). This is the metaphysical argument. Murdoch quotes Anselm:

Everything that is less good, in so far as it is good, is like the greater good. It is therefore evident to any rational mind that by ascending from the lesser good to the greater we can form a considerable notion of a being than which a greater is inconceivable. (Murdoch 1993: 394; cf. Anselm 1974: 167)

Anselm provides a way to *infer* if not to think 'something than which nothing greater can be thought' and anyone who will try to do so will realize its reality as of necessity. It is impossible to comprehend entirely 'that than which nothing greater can be thought', but it is not beyond all comprehension.[29]

Murdoch similarly attributes great importance to inferring the greater good from the lesser good, and in pursuing the metaphysical argument she suggests a return from God to Good, understanding the argument within moral philosophy:

the definition of God as non-contingent is given body by our most general perceptions and *experience* of the fundamental and omnipresent (uniquely necessary) nature of moral value, thought of in a Christian context as God. This is essentially an argument from morality not from design. It appeals to our moral understanding ... [Those] who feel perhaps that the Proof proves something, but not any sort of God, might return to Plato and claim some uniquely necessary status for moral value as something (uniquely) impossible to be thought away from human experience, and as in a special sense, if conceived of, known as real. (Murdoch 1993: 396)

Thus, Murdoch considers the proof to be about the Good rather than God. Through 'our ability to distinguish good and evil' it may prove the necessary existence of moral value. It is moreover not only rational argument, but also '[i]n learning, loving, creatively imagining, [that] we may be inspired or overcome by a sense of certainty at a particular point' (Murdoch 1993: 400). Consequently, throughout her work Murdoch urges her readers to do precisely that: to learn, to love, and to imagine. As the object of the proof also surpasses consciousness as 'a distant goal of perfection' (Antonaccio 2000: 52; cf. 128) it directs all imagination, learning, loving. Murdoch is not urging her readers merely to *imagine*, but to *imagine as well as they can*.

So, while properly imagining one has to acknowledge the presence of something that is both presumed by and surpasses one's imagination. Murdoch recognizes the proof as such in the myth of anamnesis in Plato's *Meno*. What is proven is as it were remembered, a process with which we, according to Murdoch, are all familiar (Murdoch 1993: 393). The 'belief' that the ontological proof tries to 'prove' urges itself upon anyone who is properly imagining with the certainty of something already known or intuited. By the recurring use of 'we' Murdoch urges 'us' to start imagining and thus to 'prove' what we already intuit. The 'belief' is religious yet independent of 'religions'.

The Fool

The position of the 'ordinary unbeliever or Fool' (Murdoch 1993: 410) has become rather awkward. What to think of him or her if he or she persists in denying the existence of the Good? The unbeliever must be unable or unwilling to understand, or perhaps enjoys not understanding. This fool must be either stupid, unrighteous, or a sophist, but is certainly not right and not speaking the truth.

Should this then be the final word on the fool? Such a conclusion seems incongruous with much of the tone and content of Murdoch's work. Her work is hospitable to different opinions and she is seldom wholly dismissive of positions dissimilar to her own argument. The only exceptions may be with regard to no ordinary, but learned fools, such as Nietzsche and Heidegger: 'As for Nietzsche and (late) Heidegger, roughly, I regard those great writers as essentially demonic' (Murdoch 1993: 456). 'Possibly Heidegger is Lucifer in person' (Murdoch 1997: 358). Yet, even in these strong remarks she expresses doubt ('roughly', 'possibly') and her last unfinished work was a study of Heidegger (Conradi 1997: xxi).

The fool is not that easily dismissed. When considering Le Doeuff's fool in the second chapter, it was found that she was not the only fool in the history of philosophy, but rather that philosophy has a long tradition of fools. Some of them are encountered in the reception of Anselm's ontological proof, which reveals an eagerness to identify with the fool and to argue on his behalf. Gaunilo is only the first of a larger group of distinguished thinkers. One wonders if Anselm might have come to regret the appearance of this fiction in his proof, had he realized its popularity through the centuries.

With regard to Murdoch's work too, one can feel compelled to identify with Murdoch's 'ordinary unbeliever or Fool', if not in an immediate reaction, then certainly after considering limitations in her work: limitations in her understanding of religion, the limitations in her understanding of art and the limited number of art works to which Murdoch refers in her philosophical essays, or limitations in the characters she creates in her novels. The Good may be somehow inextricably bound up with the lives and thoughts of Oxford dons and London civil servants, but is it also with the fools outside those worlds? May one assume that the proof has convinced Alcibiades, that talking about the Good is *not* just imaginary and ineffectual?

I shall remain in the role of thinker and look at the proof again, especially at the position of its fool. I shall do so by resuming the comparison of Anselm's and Murdoch's understanding of the ontological argument. As pointed out before, Anselm introduces the fool when unfolding his onto-logical proof in the second chapter of the *Proslogion*. After stating that 'we believe that thou art a being than which nothing greater can be conceived' he wonders why the fool denies God's existence (Anselm 1974: 7).

Anselm addresses the foolishness of the fool in chapter IV. Why does the fool say that there is no God? 'Why, except that he is dull and a fool?' (Anselm 1974: 9).[30] Anselm finds the solution to this riddle by means of a semantic analysis:

> There is not only one sense in which something is 'said in one's heart' or thought, for in one sense a thing is thought when the word signifying it is thought; in another sense when the very object which the thing is is under-stood. (Anselm 1974: 9–10)

In other words, the fool uses the word 'God' without giving it its proper meaning or giving it any meaning at all.[31] The fool thinks 'that than which nothing greater can be conceived', but not in the way that will lead to the conclusion of its existence.

Where does this leave Gaunilo, the first to answer Anselm? That Gaunilo is no fool becomes apparent at the last part of his answer where he suggests a correction to the proof and praises the chapters in the *Proslogion* that follow the first four (Anselm 1974: 151, 152–153). And so Anselm directs his answer to 'one who, though speaking on the Fool's behalf, is an orthodox Christian and no fool' (Anselm 1974: 153). Murdoch, significantly, calls Gaunilo 'a professional holy man' and remarks that he 'of course believed in God' (Murdoch 1993: 396 and 394 respectively). So, Anselm first replies by appealing to Gaunilo's 'faith and conscience'. The argument on the fool's foolishness thus enters an impasse once again. The fool is nothing but a regrettable fiction. Every thinker's identification with the fool is likely to lead the thinker away from the argument and from the belief in the reality of the Good.

Yet, fools are not only in the habit of turning up when least expected, they also appear in various disguises. So far it has been assumed that philosophers and their fools are completely different. Yet, this assumption can be chal-lenged. It has been argued that Anselm needs the fool in his argument, and even that the fool is indispensable in the argument.[32] The fool is needed for two different reasons: first, because of Anselm's Christian perspective and, second, for the argument's sake. Anselm starts his argument not from the perspective of an unbeliever, but instead desires to understand what he believes (*fides quaerens intellectum*). Christian belief is never questioned in the argument. Instead, the proof is considered as a step on the way to redemption, 'of re-establishing man – at least partially – in that state from which he has fallen' (Hayen 1968: 167–168).[33] This process will not be finished until all have been redeemed, not only all Christians, but also all heretics, heathens and other fools.[34] Without the fool's redemption Anselm will not be redeemed. Anselm does not direct his argument *against* the fool, but *to* the fool (Hayen 1968: 168).[35] Then again, it is not correct to conceive of Anselm as the simply righteous one who teaches the fool. Anselm's fool is no absolute stranger to him, but instead he is his own fool. The first chapter of the *Proslogion*, so often omitted in the discussion on the ontological proof, reveals Anselm's desire to see God as well as his despair at God's absence.[36] Anselm's argument is directed both to his own and to the fool's disbelief.

The second reason why Anselm needs the fool would stem from the exercise of arguing. Anselm desires to understand what he believes. His faith is never separated from the act of reasoning, yet reason is not simply enriching faith. It is seeking its own fulfilment (Hayen 1968: 174). Reason, it is argued, is for Anselm not 'a mere "faculty"', and still less, a mere abstraction called "Reason". It is the concrete existing reason' (Hayen 1968: 176). This is why Anselm allows for space for intervention of actual reasoning by the fool, but even more by Gaunilo. Anselm does not direct his reply to the fool, but to the Christian who speaks on behalf of the fool. He invites Gaunilo to *actually* reflect on his own faith and his own conscience (Hayen 1968: 176ff.). For it is in the concrete act of reasoning that reason may be fulfilled and find under the guidance of faith in 'that than which nothing greater can be conceived' the reasonable reality of 'that than which nothing greater can be conceived' (Hayen 1968: 180–181).

This last point reinforces an aspect of the proof noted before. The ontological proof is an unusual proof. It is not a proof that someone can do for another person, or force others to accept without proof. Instead, this proof one has to give to oneself. The understanding of reason seeking its own fulfilment as well as Antonaccio's assertion that the ontological proof has its starting-point in consciousness emphasize the necessarily personal aspect of this proof. Thus, both in her philosophical and her fictional writing Murdoch shows a great concern for her readers' consciousness. She often addresses them directly, urging them to use their imagination, to look at great work. In her novels, the narrative reveals the presence of an author who is continuously warning her readers not to be too enchanted and not simply to accept or indulge in the story. The last sentence of *The Philosopher's*

Pupil serves here as the most eminent example, where the narrator confesses to having had 'the assistance of a certain lady' (Murdoch 1983: 576).

However, while Anselm and Murdoch may seem to agree in relation to their fools where reasoning is concerned, their position is quite different with regard to redemption. It may be that, just as Anselm is in a way his own fool, Murdoch is not totally dissimilar to her fool. Indeed, her writing constantly confirms her doubts about her own argument.[37] Even so, Murdoch's doubt is of a fundamentally different nature. Anselm in the argument never questions the Christian faith, just his own faith or that his proof aims at reestablishing fallen man. The *Proslogion* does not end with the fourth chapter, but continues by establishing God's many qualities.

Murdoch, in contrast, does not write within a certain religious tradition. Earlier it was noted that she looks for a religion which is to remain 'if all "religions" were to blow away like mist', and in the discussion of the ontological proof it was repeatedly argued how she reformulates notions so as to make them comprehensible outside the religious tradition from which she retrieves them. The difference between Anselm and Murdoch then is created by yet another fool: the fool or madman who took his lantern one bright morning and looked for God in a market place. The people around him were not upset or angry with him, but merely amused. They laughed and made fun of his quest. The fool called out: 'Where is God? . . . I'll tell you! *We have killed him* – you and I! We are all his murderers' (Nietzsche, *Gay Science* 125). Between Anselm and Murdoch one discerns the proclaimed death of God, proclaimed, that is, by a fool.

Addressing a fool who killed God would considerably change the proof. Murdoch sometimes suggests that God has to be created in order for him to exist, as for example in the quoted words of Valéry who, Murdoch argues, 'with poetic, and spiritual, inspiration in mind, says that "the proper, unique and perpetual object of thought is that which does not exist." . . . And, "At its highest point, love is a determination to create that being which it has taken for its object"' (Murdoch 1993: 401).[38] Yet, even though Murdoch uses the phrase 'the death of God' in the 1987-introduction to *Sartre: Romantic Rationalist*, it has already been noted that her language generally suggests a different metaphor, not that of the death of God, but rather of what Hillis Miller calls the disappearance of God.[39] By speaking of 'the *collapse* of religion', or of religion as 'waning rapidly', Murdoch expresses her preference for the gradual disappearance of God over his violent and abrupt death.

Yet, even if Murdoch prefers the metaphor of disappearance, she will address a fool who claims to have killed God. Would such a fool accept the

Good? Alcibiades, who castrated the gods, mockingly questions whether the Good loves Plato as much as Plato loves the Good. His question recalls 'someone's' objection in 'On "God" and "Good"' that God at least gave some consolation, whereas the Good can appeal to none but the most mystically minded (Murdoch 1997: 358; cf. 360). The fool standing between Anselm and Murdoch slowly drains her world of any promise. The imagery that Murdoch applies to the Good often emphasizes its negating nature: the Good encountered at the end of all image-making is the abyss into which one falls (Murdoch 1993: 320, 464); it is not easy to imagine what it is like to look into the sun, in Plato's allegory of the cave, and Murdoch supposes that 'to look at the sun is to be gloriously dazzled and to see nothing' (Murdoch 1997: 357); *Metaphysics as a Guide to Morals* significantly ends with a last chapter called 'The Void' (cf. Antonaccio 1996: 136–137). Given such imagery would the fool not be justified in concluding that 'it looks like religious and moral anorexia all round'? (Loades 1999: 94–95). Can such a negating Good feed the imagination?

The doubts of the fool Murdoch cannot entirely abandon, and yet, they need not be the last word. If Murdoch's philosophy indeed takes place in a 'huge hall of reflection', it is possible to imagine how in such a hall aunties and servants will be lingering in the corners, simply having faith – even faith in the fool who declares that God is dead. Moreover, the various works of art Murdoch returns to throughout her work still testify to imagination's strength. Murdoch often points out how in thinking, imagining, loving anyone can prove the proof of the necessary existence of the Good as the structuring principle of consciousness and reality. In order to do so it may be enough to be deeply in love with Socrates. Murdoch has given unreligious believers a variety of possibilities for proving the ontological proof. She has thus reintroduced an absolute value in her imaginative philosophy, even if it is only for those who want to believe.

The doubts of even a half convinced fool are, I would conclude, directly related to Murdoch's idiosyncratic way of reading texts. I have come to regard Murdoch's idiosyncratic position as both the strength and the weakness of her work. The idiosyncrasy shows in various ways: in her understanding of literature, her reading of Kant, her understanding of religion, her appreciation of Plato. In taking art rather than science as a model for philosophy, Murdoch has taken a direction different from that of many of her contemporaries in philosophy.

While her idiosyncrasy may be justifiably criticized, one should not do so without acknowledging its positive features. Murdoch has been severely criticized for her understanding of literature, yet I have shown that it enabled her to take an original position in contemporary philosophy and challenge various presuppositions held without much consideration. Most important here is the distinction between fact and value. Her reading of Kant ignores more generally held concerns, but it has enabled her to place imagination in the centre of our consciousness. Her unusual interest in Plato has enabled her to posit an understanding of imagination that is not exalted, while also retaining or reintroducing the Good as an absolute standard in philosophy. Her reading of religion may disregard and misinterpret various aspects of the Christian religion, but it has enabled her to describe a form of contemplation that she considers open for everyone.

Yet, Murdoch's idiosyncratic position also involves withdrawing from contemporary discussions and works. This I find creates an emptiness in her thought. Murdoch attempts to find a timeless form of attention, which she recognizes in both the Christian religion and Plato. Even though she sometimes remarks on being a child of her time, she also removes herself from contemporary discussions and works of art and presents her readings and preferences as unqualified. Of course, such remarks should not entirely be taken at face value. Moreover, this attitude does not make her position timeless, and it is easily possible to relate her preference for Tolstoy and Shakespeare, her interest in character and her understanding of religion to various stages of her (British, Oxford, philosophical) education. Thus one may argue that Murdoch is more culturally determined than she admits to being. More importantly, however, I find that this preference for such timeless attention weakens her argument and remove some of its intensity. In preferring the universal to the actual Murdoch at times appears as a philosopher who has only just returned to the cave and whose eyes still need to adjust to the darkness. This philosopher can make general observations about the particularity of things and may urge contemplation of these, but one is waiting for the eyes to adjust even more, to see the particulars themselves, their relation to one another, their history and possibilities.

Conclusion

This chapter returns to the question 'How can we make ourselves morally better?' This is the central question of Murdoch's philosophy. 'How can we make ourselves morally better?' and not, for instance, 'Why should we make ourselves morally better?' Murdoch does not have much interest in the political background to 'How can we make ourselves morally better?' Moreover, for Murdoch, making oneself morally better is not rewarded in a traditional sense.

In 'Above the Gods' the political consequences of God's disappearance are noted, but quickly put aside. Instead, the discussion turns to what the disappearance means for individuals in relation to some independent reality. Murdoch looks, as young Plato puts it, for a morality that is so serious, that it is religious. Yet, religious does not refer here to any 'religion' in particular here, just as faith does not refer here to any particular faith. Murdoch provides the unreligious believers with faith with an ontological proof for the existence of the Good rather than God.

Despite the emphasis on imagination and the use of much imagery Murdoch's world may seem rather depleted. By emphasizing the timeless and universal, but also empty character of the Good, it may lose its attraction for all but the most mystically minded. There is no final reward for being good. There is only the incentive to use one's imagination, and to use it for the Good.

Coda

Women and Philosophy

In 1929 Virginia Woolf cursed a famous library. She was in Oxbridge one fine October morning and had been walking and thinking. As she found herself near the library she decided to have a look at the manuscript that had been the object of her thought. Yet, at the door, her stream of thought was stopped by the black flutter of a gentleman in a gown: 'ladies [were] only admitted to the library if accompanied by a Fellow of the College or furnished with a letter of introduction.' Taken aback, Woolf muses: 'That a famous library has been cursed by a woman is a matter of complete indifference to a famous library' (Woolf 1957: 8–9).

Of course, it is impossible to say whether something like this really happened. *A Room of One's Own* is fiction. 'But we asked you to talk about women and fiction', it begins. Did anyone really utter that objection? Certainly, Woolf was asked to talk about women and fiction, on two different occasions, and the lectures she gave formed the basis for *A Room of One's Own*. But did somebody really stop her from entering the library? And *who* was actually stopped? Did this person have sole and partridge for lunch, and soup and beef for dinner?

Woolf reassures her reader of the truth of her narration. 'Fiction must stick to facts, and the truer the facts the better the fiction – so we are told' (Woolf 1957: 16). Le Doeuff quotes these words in *Hipparchia's Choice*, her *Essay Concerning Women, Philosophy, etc.*, adding: 'I beg the reader to note that no similarity between the fruits of my imagination and real situations is accidental' (Le Doeuff 1991: xiii). Sixty years after the publication of *A Room of One's Own* it is still necessary to tell the story of women and knowledge. Black flutter may no longer be able to prevent a woman from entering a famous library, but it has not yet fully disappeared. The relationship between women and knowledge, between women and philosophy, is still problematic. The relationship is, as Le Doeuff argues throughout her oeuvre, troubled by an imaginary. 'Myths', she argues in *The Sex of Knowledge* 'regulate our relationship with various modes of knowledge' (Le Doeuff

2003: x). Myths about feminine intuition and myths that diminish the intellectual women of the past – discarding for instance Christine de Pisan for being 'one of the most dyed-in-the-wool blue-stocking our literature has ever known' – are damaging in this respect (Le Doeuff 2003: 5ff. and ix respectively).[1]

Yet, how to tell the continuing story of women and the library? *A Room of One's Own* is fact and fiction. Woolf was never allowed to go to university, because all the family's money was spent on her brothers' education. Yet, she did not want her critics to censure the book for complaining about personal misery (Lee 1997: 556). *A Room of One's Own* is not about anyone in particular, and that makes it a book about many. The 'biographical fantasy' of Shakespeare's sister at the centre of the book is, as Lee argues in her biography, 'at once historical and Utopian, a tragic description of what women's lives have been like and an empowering fantasy of how they might become different' (Lee 1997: 15). *A Room of One's Own* asks if women should want to enter the library. Woolf's answer to that question is ambiguous. Never having been allowed to go to university, she took pride in her position as outsider, in reading as a 'common' rather than a learned reader.[2]

Less than ten years after *A Room of One's Own* was first published a group of young women entered that same famous library. The doors of the library opened for them, and with enviable self-confidence they sat down, took part in discussions and began to write books, which would add to the existing collection. For Elizabeth Anscombe, Philippa Foot, Mary Midgley, Iris Murdoch, and Mary Warnock it seemed no more than accepted that they should take a seat, and start reading, writing, teaching – in short earn their living as philosophers.

Does it matter that these philosophers were women? Does it matter that Murdoch was a woman? No interviewer ever asked Murdoch about women and philosophy, but it seems unlikely that she would judge that relationship to be any different from the relationship between men and philosophy. In Chapter 2 I argued that Murdoch explicitly refused to assume the – what she deemed – particular position of woman with regard to her novels, and it is safe to assume that she would not do so either with regard to her philosophical writing. Philosophy has often been defined as a quest for universal truth. Such a quest, it is assumed, cannot start from a gendered position. By emphasizing their gender women risk locking themselves out of the library.

And yet, of the women just mentioned Murdoch presents a remarkable case study for considering persistent questions around the relation between women and knowledge, and women and philosophy. She is probably the best known, in particular outside academia. She is also the only one not to have pursued any lengthy academic career. Her appointment at St Anne's lasted 14 years, and preceded the publication of her best-known philosophical works: *The Sovereignty of Good* (1970), *The Fire and the Sun* (1976) and *Metaphysics as a Guide to Morals* (1992).

I have argued that especially in her earlier writing, when still at St Anne's, Murdoch often positions herself as an outsider. She makes a clear distinction between the philosophical argument and 'us', 'when we are not philosophising' (Murdoch 1997: 33). The claim to speak from an ordinary position keeps returning in her philosophical writing up to and including 'The Idea of Perfection'. In that essay Murdoch explains the example of M and D 'as yet without justification', when she finds herself once again defied by philosophical argument (Murdoch 1997: 316). Murdoch first presented 'The Idea of Perfection' at the Ballard Matthews lecture in 1962, the year she decided to resign from St Anne's (Conradi 2001b: 647 n. 59).

In later works Murdoch gradually stops positioning her ideas explicitly in opposition to philosophical argument, but the importance of the ordinary remains. It is found in the frequent use of words like 'simple', 'surely' and 'obvious', as well as by acknowledging those outside the philosophical debate: the virtuous peasants, 'some quiet unpretentious worker, a school-teacher, or a mother, or better still an aunt'. And, Murdoch claims, 'I have known such aunts (Murdoch 1993: 429). Of course, these examples are not necessarily simple. And they are also fiction.

In the reception of her philosophical work, Murdoch has indeed remained somewhat of an outsider, as Widdows rightly points out. Her work rarely appears on the reading lists of postgraduate courses, let alone undergraduate ones. Widdows attributes this omission to the fact that Murdoch was not part of the mainstream philosophical traditions of her time, and that her writing is not easy to understand (Widdows 2005: 10). In the first chapter I discussed how Murdoch's choice of topics indeed differed from those of mainstream British philosophy. Her first book was on Sartre, whose writings were of little interest to most of her contemporaries in Oxford. Murdoch's subsequent interest in religion, and in value, singled her out again. In addition, one could mention her unusual double oeuvre of novels and philosophical writing.

But, you may argue, what does this have to do with gender? Even if it took some time and effort before Murdoch received recognition as a philosopher, this delay does not need to be in any way related to her being a woman. In other words, why bring Woolf into this discussion? The best and certainly the shortest reply would be, why not? It is not necessary to decide whether there is such a thing as female nature in order to claim that women have been and still are treated differently from men. Gender matters in philosophy, as long as there are anthologies that introduce Sartre with references to his books, while De Beauvoir's friendships, relationships and affairs are listed (Moran and Mooney 2006: 377–381 and 463–466).[3]

The question if and how Murdoch's gender matters has often been in my mind when working on this research. While I was pondering her philosophical ideas, a discussion went on in the newspapers and in books about her personal life: her friendships, relationships, and affairs – by which some people claimed to have been shocked – and her loss of mind when suffering from Alzheimer's disease in the last years of her life. Murdoch's husband John Bayley published three autobiographical memoirs, and two competing biographies claimed to present the real Iris. And then there was the film, *Iris*, with its curious tagline 'Her greatest talent was for life'. Gender seemed to matter in these discussions, as a woman was once again defined by her body. Or was this interest nothing but the usual gossip that follows a wake? Is it a judgement on her work, that Oxford decided to honour Murdoch by naming a chair in Old Age Psychiatry after her? In recent years – and this is fact, not fiction – I have heard lectures at academic conferences, which solely featured anecdotes from Murdoch's life – and not the most flattering ones for all that – not mentioning her work at all until the last minute.[4]

There are even better reasons to consider the question of women and philosophy in relation to Murdoch. Murdoch was one of the first women to pursue a career in a discipline that previously had been the prerogative of a privileged group of men. Now, almost ten years after her death, libraries admit many more people who in earlier times were not even anywhere near them – women and men of different classes, and of different social, cultural, and religious backgrounds. Even though these women and men are trained in the existing tradition, the norms and practices that used to be regarded as self-evident and neutral are being challenged in different ways. There is, moreover, a growing body of literature on these issues. Feminist philosophers, for instance, have questioned the persistent elitism of their discipline. There is no reason why these new insights could not be applied to Murdoch, or even to suggestions such as the one made by Warnock in her memoirs that 'women are . . . more reluctant to abandon common sense'.[5]

Common sense may indeed have introduced the multiple use of 'obvious' and 'surely' into Murdoch's philosophy. It may also have created the dialogical nature of her writing, by suggesting to Murdoch that one is rarely alone in a room near the fire.[6] I have argued that Murdoch's philosophical argument is habitually interrupted by various voices, who challenge and question her. Moreover, these challenges are not always silenced. Instead, Murdoch admits to being 'often more than half persuaded to think' in the terms of her challengers, and yet she wants to stay with her own point and to be convinced by it (Murdoch 1997: 359). Murdoch's philosophical argument is not made by a lonely individual, but by one who knows of people around her.[7]

Yet, despite Warnock's suggestion, these idiosyncrasies in Murdoch's philosophical writing are not necessarily those of a woman. Murdoch quotes Moore, when she suggests a return 'towards the consideration of simple and obvious facts' (Murdoch 1997: 299). Her preference for simplicity can thus be seen as merely part of a particular philosophical tradition. The plea for simplicity and the dialogical nature can also be considered idiosyncrasies typical of a novelist. It has indeed been argued that Murdoch is a novelist, even when she is writing philosophy. Murdoch describes for instance the problem central to her philosophy in terms of novel writing: the image of the good person is that of a novelist creating characters. The various virtuous peasants also seem to come straight out of the nineteenth-century novels she favours so much, rather than out of life. Moreover, Murdoch habitually describes the various philosophical disputes as battles, or unlikely weddings. Yet, the importance of literature does not imply that Murdoch is only a novelist. As I argued in Chapter 3, philosophy and literature blend in Murdoch's writing. She is at times a novelist when doing philosophy, but she is also, conversely, a philosopher when writing her novels – expressing, for instance, a *metaphysical* regret about the discrepancy between the messiness of reality and the structuring elements of thought when writing novels (Byatt 1994: 216–217).

Then again, calling Murdoch a novelist when attempting to characterize her philosophy does not necessarily avoid the issue of gender. Literature has been one of the very few intellectual professions that have been open for women for some time. Women were writers before they were allowed to enter university and become doctors, lawyers, or philosophers, and there have been, of course, some very famous novelists, especially in England. Thus, by equating common sense and literature Murdoch may be understood to become part of a tradition of women who wrote literature, but were still outside the academic discourse of philosophy, outside the library. For Murdoch, this tradition of women writers may have been more dear and more familiar than the one in the library that she had just entered. Indeed, it has been her achievement to let the two meet.

To claim that Murdoch's writing style singles her out as a woman reintroduces a perennial feminist dilemma. In order to find recognition for values that are not generally recognized, one has to use those distinctions that one wants to abolish. Thus, the need to argue that certain values have been associated with women for a long time, and that they have not been given much esteem. Yet, reclaiming the notions as female may risk continuing existing inequality. I would argue that it is no coincidence that a surprising number of women philosophers write on imagination and on literature. Philosophers like Nussbaum, Murdoch and Arendt each in their own way attach great importance to fiction and to literature. They provide, moreover, good reasons for doing so. However, this coincidence does not imply that *only women* can write about literature and imagination, or that women can *only* write about literature and imagination. And yet, it is necessary to notice the gender of these thinkers, for the notions of imagination and the imaginary have too often been disregarded in the history of philosophy.

It is then important to call Murdoch a woman *and* a philosopher. Of course, one hesitates to do so, because Murdoch herself would have resented it. However, her objections were directed against being singled out for being a woman. In other words, she objected to singling out as a means of exclusion. Yet, calling Murdoch a woman and a philosopher could create inclusion, and recognition of diversity. Moreover, it would counter the focus on her personal life. Murdoch was not just a woman when she lived her life and lost her mind. She was also a woman when she wrote and thought and taught. Moreover, the woman philosopher Murdoch would allow for rewriting the history of philosophy, as women have started to rewrite history.[8] Next to the history where she sides with Plato, Sartre, Kant and Wittgenstein, there could be one where she *as a philosopher* sides with – who knows – Woolf, George Eliot, Christine de Pisan?[9] It would be a history of outsiders, who were also insiders. A history of fiction to tell the facts. Just as for Plato, philosophy would rise again out of literature.

Notes

1 Introduction

1. See Fletcher and Bove (1994) for a complete list of works published until 1994. The bibliography in this book contains a selection, including more recent work.
2. For some it is even 'the central problem which Iris Murdoch's work poses for us ...: is she a novelist-philosopher or a novelist *and* a philosopher? In other words, is there a relationship between her novels and her philosophy and if so, what is this relationship?' (Question posed by Le Gros, in Chevalier (1978: 63), as quoted and translated by Spear (1995: 7).)
3. Compare for example the following two quotations from *The Black Prince* and 'On "God" and "Good"' respectively: 'What does he fear? is usually the key to the artist's mind' (Murdoch 1973: 85) and '(It is always a significant question to ask about any philosopher: what is he afraid of?)' (Murdoch 1997: 359). All references to Murdoch's essays use the collection *Existentialists and Mystics: Writings on Philosophy and Literature* (1997) unless indicated differently. This includes references to *The Fire and the Sun, The Sovereignty of Good*, as well as the interview with Magee, 'Philosophy and Literature: A Conversation with Bryan Magee'.
4. I am referring here to the first line of *Nuns and Soldiers* (1980). The count, who hears the dying man, is surprised, not so much because Wittgenstein is mentioned, but because Wittgenstein is challenged at the last minute.
5. See, for example, Murdoch (1997: 294–5). Murdoch has been criticized for evaluating literature in moral terms, especially by Wood (1999). See also Chapter 4.
6. In Chapter 3 I argue that this concerns in particular the portrayal of characters in her novels. Conradi (2001a) considers her novels to do so, whereas Bergonzi (1979) thinks they don't. Compare Chapter 3.
7. See for the former O'Connell (1996) and for the latter Willemsen (1998).
8. Byatt (1994: 208). Byatt also rightly remarks: 'Reviewers have talked a great deal about whether Miss Murdoch is or is not a "philosophical novelist"; those who say she is not tend to describe her as a compulsive storyteller, which is not of course incompatible with being a philosophical novelist' (Byatt 1994: 207).
9. See Nussbaum (1986b: 16). In *Love's Knowledge* Nussbaum repeats her argument, but adds that she cannot understand how these statements relate to Murdoch's own thoughts (Nussbaum 1990: 251 and note 8). Cf. Antonaccio (2000: 19–20 and 199 n. 58), and see also Nussbaum (1996: 29–53).

10. See in particular the first pages of 'The Sovereignty of Good Over Other Concepts' (Murdoch 1997: 363ff.). See also Chapter 2.
11. Compare in this respect Antonaccio's notion of 'reflexive realism', to be discussed in the next part.
12. Interview with Le Gros in Chevalier (1978: 79), as quoted in Spear (1995: 8).
13. Her reluctance to call herself a real philosopher is perhaps even better portrayed in the comic image of pupils of the philosopher Dave Gellman in *Under the Net* to whom

> the world is a mystery; a mystery to which it should be reasonably possible to dis-cover a key. The key would be something of the sort that could be contained in a book of some eight hundred pages. To find the key would not necessarily be a simple matter, but Dave's pupils feel sure that the dedication of between four and ten hours a week, excluding University vacations, should suffice to find it. (Murdoch 1954: 25)

14. Byatt (1994: 207); Spear (1995: 23–24). See also Spear (1995: 121):

> One problem is that she defies classification: she is not a Modernist; she is not a Post-Modernist; she is not, like many of her female contemporaries, a feminist writer; yet, despite the fact that she employs many Victorian devices in her novels, no serious reader of her fiction could place her among the traditionalists.

15. See the various biting remarks by his fellow author Bradley Pearson, and in parti-cular the review of Baffin's latest book (Murdoch 1973: 151–2). For a concise out-line of the development of Murdoch's novels in different periods, as well as a description of returning imagery, see also Todd (1994/5).
16. Backus phrases his general objection as follows:

> ... to locate, as a general principle, the controlling intention in a work of art or philosophy squarely with the artist is mistaken. Heidegger's compelling accounts of Descartes as preoccupied with Being and Nietzsche as the last metaphysicians of the West, Derrida's story of Husserl as a protogrammatologist: these interpre-tations are falsification enough. (Backus 1986: 13)

17. See also Conradi (2001b), with the curious title 'Did Iris Murdoch Draw from Life?' and a presentation at the first Iris Murdoch Conference: 'On Writing *Iris Murdoch: A Life*: Freud versus Multiplicity', 1st Annual Conference of the Iris Murdoch Society, St Anne's Oxford, 14 September 2002.
18. As noted for instance by Lievers (2001).
19. Warnock writes how Ayer 'was the only person (apart from Iris) who was credited with any knowledge of [the existentialists'] philosophy; and I remember a pecu-liarly dismissive talk he gave in the Oxford Playhouse, to introduce a translated version of *Huis Clos* that was being staged there' (Warnock 2000: 91).
20. Arguing the historical as well as contemporary importance of Murdoch's criticism of the distinction between fact and value, Diamond mentions H. Putnam, *Realism with a Human Face* (1990) as one who regards *The Sovereignty of Good* as 'groundbreak-ing in this regard' (Diamond 1996: 104 n. 22).

21. That is, the last work published. Murdoch was writing a work on Heidegger, which she abandoned when she became ill (Conradi 1997: xxi).

22. The excerpt from *The Book and the Brotherhood* is quoted in Hacking (1992).

23. O'Connell, *To Love the Good* (1996) omits Murdoch's last and largest work, *Metaphysics as a Guide to Morals*. The argument in the present book was formed before the publication of Widdows (2005), and refers to the work only occasionally. Laverty (2007) was published when the manuscript of the present book was practically finished. I regret that I am unable to engage with it here.

24. See for the importance of Schweiker for this work p. 197 n. 35. Antonaccio refers here to Schweiker's *Responsibility and Christian Ethics* (1995: 106–114), and admits to being deeply influenced by it. Schweiker, in his turn, confesses to borrowing terms from Taylor. See Schweiker (1995: 114), as well as chapters seven and eight. He refers to Taylor's *Sources of the Self* (1989) in particular its 23rd chapter and its conclusion, and to Taylor's 'Responsibility for Self' (1982).

25. See Antonaccio (2000: 15 and 123ff.). For a more elaborate discussion of the ontological proof see Chapter 5.

26. This persuasion is repeated at the beginning of almost every chapter. Compare with the beginning of chapter three, where Antonaccio recapitulates 'the book's general thesis that the importance of Murdoch's thought for contemporary ethics lies in her effort to redescribe the moral self and its integral relation to the good' (Antonaccio 2000: 61). Compare too the first pages of chapters four, five and six.

27. Ordinary Language Man and Totalitarian Man appear in 'The Sublime and the Beautiful Revisited' (Murdoch 1997: 268–270).

28. Antonaccio (2000: 23). The quotation is taken from 'Metaphysics and Ethics' (Murdoch 1997: 74).

29. This questions are raised in 'On "God" and "Good"' (Murdoch 1997: 342). Compare 'The Sovereignty of Good Over Other Concepts' (Murdoch 1997: 364 and 368). Murdoch uses 'man' when speaking of the whole human race. In Chapter 2 it is argued that she considers the position of 'man' to be universal, whereas 'woman' is not. I do not comment on this use of these words apart from the designated pages in Chapter 2. In my own writing I try to avoid using concepts that apply to considerably fewer people than intended. The difficulty of language's inclusiveness and exclusiveness is not easily solved. In general, I believe that creativity often provides a better solution than using either exclusive language (often with a reference to grammar) or inclusive language, where there is no inclusion. (Substituting male examples with females does not always solve the problem of inclusiveness.)

30. See Diamond on the importance of Murdoch's criticism of the distinction between fact and value. Diamond points out that Murdoch was one of the first to criticize 'two closely related ideas', 'accepted as virtually unquestionable' in the 1950s: 'that it is a logical error to attempt to infer any evaluative conclusion from factual premises, and that there is a fundamental distinction between fact and value' (Diamond 1996: 79). In the conclusion of this part Diamond outlines points where Murdoch's work is still relevant for contemporary analytical philosophy, mentioning in particular her understanding of fiction.

31. Murdoch (1997: 363–364). In the earlier discussion of the notion of 'reflexive realism' it was argued that this notion of 'realism' can be understood in different ways, hence the quotation marks around the word in the subsequent sentences. See also the discussion of realism in Chapter 4.

32. The image of cricket playing and cake eating is taken from *Sartre: Romantic Rationalist* (Murdoch 1999: 78–79). It is a description of Ryle's *The Concept of Mind*.

33. See also Chapter 3, in particular the discussion of M and D.

34. Murdoch (1997: 341). In recent years several works have provided an account of Murdoch's ambiguous relationship with Freud and psychoanalysis. Turner (1993) provides a psychoanalytic reading of eight of Murdoch's novels. Turner distinguishes different reasons why Murdoch distances herself from Freud so strictly: she would distrust the emphasis put on introspection, fearing that the other will disappear in this process. In addition, Turner argues, '[Freud], too, is a father-figure she is emulating and castrating in order to be effective as herself' (Turner 1993: 12). This last remark indicates the disappointing turn the readings of Murdoch's novels take. Based on admittedly sparse biographical information Turner reads Murdoch's novels from assumptions about the relationship between her and her parents. I find his readings rather forced. Turner decidedly ignores possible arguments against Freudian ideas in favour of personal analysis.

35. And yet, hardly any quotation from Murdoch's novels unambiguously reaffirms her philosophical position. Here, I wonder whether the bishop's gluttony is a reflection on Murdoch's all-too eager dismissal of Christian imagery.

36. This is the title of one novel, which features the rectory of an atheist priest isolated from the world by permanent fog. It is also a term used in *The Philosopher's Pupil* to characterize the present era (Murdoch 1983: 187).

37. Jansen (2001: 61). The quotations are taken from Dipple (1982: 3), Ramanathan (1990: 23) and Hawkins (1993: 91).

38. The three areas distinguished are 'the area in which imagination is linked with *image* and image is understood as *mental image* ... the area in which imagination is associated with invention and the area in which imagination is linked with false belief'. In the remainder of the article he intends to connect Kant's use of imagination in *The Critique of Pure Reason* to perceptual recognition (Strawson 1971: 31, italics in original).

39. See, for example, 'On "God" and "Good"', where the imperative 'consider' urges the reader to look at Velasquez or Titian, or to read Shakespeare or Tolstoy. See Chapter 4 for a more thorough discussion (Murdoch 1997: 353).

2 Philosophy and Its Imagery

1. I have consulted mainly the interviews collected in Dooley (2003). See in particular the interviews with Hale (pp. 30–32), Bellamy (pp. 44–55), Biles (pp. 56–69), Chevalier (pp. 70–96), Brans (pp. 155–166) and Heusel (pp. 194–208).

2. Dooley (2003: 5 and 207, respectively). Hobson in fact exposes Murdoch to some of his own sexist views, as I have argued elsewhere (Altorf 2006: 175).

3. Griffin (1993: 2); cf. Backus (1986: 13).

4. For a discussion of these works up to 1993, see Griffin (1993: 7–13). See also Grimshaw (2005).

5. Exceptions should be made for the use of Murdoch's philosophical writing in the context of care ethics. *The Oxford Handbook of Aesthetics* (Levinson 2003: 647–666) also mentions Murdoch's work as a possible subject for further research.

6. Dooley (2003: 32, italics in original). Grimshaw also notes Murdoch's high regard for De Beauvoir. Yet, I think it significant that while Grimshaw provides an interpretation of Murdoch's novels through *The Second Sex*, Murdoch's understanding of this work is rarely mentioned (Grimshaw 2005: 74–116).

7. Midgley did write about feminism. See her *Women's Choices: Philosophical Problems Facing Feminism* (1983) with Judith Hughes. This work does not acknowledge a change in philosophical reasoning as a consequence of women becoming philosophers, but rather a change in topics.

8. It should be noted that in other texts, Nussbaum has questioned rationality, and criticized philosophy for failing to understand the importance of emotion. This has been a permanent recurring theme in her work since *The Fragility of Goodness* (1986).

9. For an extensive selection of philosophical writings about women (from Laotse, Konfuzius and Demokritos to Horkheimer, Marcuse and Gehlen), see Stopczyk (1980).

10. Le Doeuff argues that philosophy projects its unavoidable use of imagery on an 'Other ... the child (in that we have all been one, before becoming ... a man!), nursery stories, the people (irrational by nature), old wives' tales, folklore, etc.' (Le Doeuff 1989: 6).

11. Then again, the readings of, for example, Griffin and Johnson testify that her novels do not simply approve of this situation.

12. Murdoch (1993: 305). Cf. Brugmans (2004: 5ff.).

13. For instance, Antonaccio's approach of conceptual hermeneutics allows for the possibility of translation of the picture of M and D into non-metaphorical components, as 'examples' that 'illuminate' ideas presented (Antonaccio 2000: 21ff., 87ff.). Similarly, Kant's philosophy as well as the 'stern picture of solitary all-responsible man' can be and has been described in non-metaphorical elements. It would seem that, contrary to what Murdoch argues, philosophy can do without these images.

14. When translating *The Sovereignty of Good* into Dutch, Mariëtte Willemsen and I were struck by these images. This part owes much to the discussions we had. See also Altorf and Willemsen (2003: 24).

15. I am not the first to compare Murdoch's philosophy, and especially her last and largest work, to her novels or to myth. (See for instance Hacking 1992.)

16. Indeed, Le Doeuff has been criticized by certain feminist thinkers for using the term imaginary the way she does. It has been argued that Le Doeuff's use of

the term 'imaginary' is vague, and does not provide 'a reading position in relation to the whole', or a 'stable reference point' (Morris 1981–82: 72), (as quoted in Maras (2000: 87)). Maras contributes the assumed vagueness of the notion, as for instance noted by Grosz and Morris, to unfortunate translations of the term *l'imagier*.

17. See, for example, the opening paragraphs of the other two essays that together with 'The Sovereignty of Good Over Other Concepts' make up Murdoch's best-known philosophical work *The Sovereignty of Good*. In 'The Idea of Perfection' Murdoch mentions those 'musts' in which 'lie the deepest springs and motives of philosophy'. Murdoch lists two: 'Contemporary philosophers frequently connect consciousness with virtue, and although they constantly talk of freedom they rarely talk of love. But there must be some relation between these latter concepts, and it must be possible to do justice to both Socrates and the virtuous peasant' (Murdoch 1997: 299–300). 'On "God" and "Good"' starts thus: 'To do philosophy is to explore one's own temperament, and yet at the same time to attempt to discover the truth' (Murdoch 1997: 337).

18. See also La Caze (2000: 71). Although La Caze uses the word 'method' when applying it to images in analytical philosophy she notes that 'it would not work if one were simply to imitate her method'.

19. Le Doeuff (1989: 3). Le Doeuff explains the difference between her work and two perspectives of *thinking in images*:

> Our time has seen major studies of myth and dream, locations where thought in images is in some sense at home. Bachelard, conversely, has offered analysis of the imaginary component within scientific work, whose final aim is to extradite an element judged alien and undesirable, and assign it a residence *elsewhere*. The perspective I am adopting here differs, as will be seen, from both these approaches, since it involves reflecting on strands of the imaginary operating in places where, in principle, they are supposed not to belong and yet where, without them, nothing would have been accomplished. (Le Doeuff 1989: 2)

20. In a footnote Le Doeuff suggests: 'This successive order should not be taken as a hard-and-fast rule. Let us say that there are several complementary ways of approaching the image ... The interpretation of the image lies at the intersection of these different areas of investigation' (Le Doeuff 1989: 172 n. 10). Le Doeuff illustrates these four by discussing a passage from Kant. In chapter III of book II of the *Critique of Pure Reason* Kant sums up what has been achieved so far and imme-diately introduces the image of an island to which he compares 'the territory of pure understanding', which has been 'explored', 'carefully surveyed' and 'measured' in the preceding text (Kant, *Critique of Pure Reason*, A235–236/B295–296; Le Doeuff 1989: 8ff.).

21. The analytical tradition, interestingly enough, may be suspicious of the use of metaphors, but does not conceal the use of examples. Compare here La Caze: 'The image or imaginary anecdote is displayed rather than hidden by the analyti-cal philosopher, but the blatant use of fantasy as a method of uncovering allegedly

necessary conceptual truths distracts attention from the assumptions made by the way the story is told' (La Caze 2000: 67).

22. With respect to the example she uses Le Doeuff wonders whether Kant has only one island or does he speak of various ones, and how do they relate to one another (Le Doeuff 1989: 9)? A second, southern island is found in *Conjectural Beginning of Human History* (1786).

23. Both in her article 'Ants and Women, or Philosophy without Borders' and in the interview with Mortley she relates an occasion on which she gave a paper on Bacon, where someone in the audience noted the inaccuracies about ants, but no one mentioned those about women. Le Doeuff concludes: 'I have come to the conclusion that insects are more protected against philosophical abuse than women' (Mortley 1991: 86–87; Le Doeuff 1987: 41).

24. For Aristippus Le Doeuff refers to Diogenes Laertius' *Lives and Opinions of Eminent Philosophers* (1925: 98–102). Deutscher does not use this exact quotation from *Hipparchia's Choice*, but offers an abbreviated quote from the longer section, leaving out some of the more scathing remarks.

25. See Janik (1998: 1–22), on different kinds of fools.

26. Anselm's ontological proof is discussed at length in Chapter 5. There I also argue that the fool does not necessarily present the opposite of Anselm.

27. In the interview with Mortley, Le Doeuff remarks that the imaginary is indeed a unifying theme, adding:

> Some people find it strange that I sometimes work on imaginary islands, utopias, or the idea of the island of reason, for example, and sometimes on the representation of women in philosophical texts. I can't see why they wonder, since it is one and the same approach in a sense ... My work is about the stock of images you can find in philosophical works, whatever they refer to: insect, clocks, women, or islands. I try to show what part they play in the philosophical enterprise. But, obviously, when I work on the figure of 'woman', something more important is at stake than when I work on imaginary islands. (Mortley 1991: 85–86)

28. Le Doeuff (1991: 9). In a footnote Le Doeuff mentions 'one woman with a clown's inspiration in Shakespeare's work and that is Beatrice in *Much Ado about Nothing*. What she challenges is the touchy pride of the play's male protagonists and its effects on the position of women. We who have been involved in feminism are all Beatrices' (Le Doeuff 1991: 318 n. 9).

29. See Janik (1998: 13), who argues that the fool subverts the opposition between masculinity and femininity, and does not replace the one with the other.

30. Compare too:

> we do not think that feminism is an operation by which 'woman' wants to be like 'man', we insist on the fact that there are *women*, quite different from each other, and that there are *men* also. 'Woman' is a smoke-screen which prevents people from seeing the actual situations of real women. (Le Doeuff 1987: 49)

31. In this respect he resembles women, as suggested by Le Doeuff in the interview with Mortley (Mortley 1991: 85).

32. In various performances of *King Lear* the Fool was left out, because he was considered indecorous. Some of these performances also ended with the wedding of Edgar and Cordelia. See Hager (1998: 293).

33. Alcoff remarks on this distinction, made by various feminists. Among them is Braidotti, who, Alcoff argues, 'uses [it], so that she can position herself in the vanguard rebellious camp. However, Alcoff doubts whether this distinction applies to every woman. 'Perhaps our female status as the disinherited may free us from any dialectic of the sons oscillating between loyalty and rebellion, and will make it possible to create a new relationship to the fathers, less caught in binaries, more capable of independence.' (Alcoff 1995: 77 n. 18)

34. As Sartre took De Beauvoir. See Le Doeuff (1991: 137ff.).

3   Literature, Character and Philosophy

1. The analytical philosophy that Murdoch encountered she also calls 'linguistic analysis' and 'linguistic behaviourism' (cf. Antonaccio 2000: 205 n. 2).

2. Cf. Murdoch (1997: 266–267), where literature is said to give 'a more telling diagnosis of these ills [i.e. of philosophy]' and (1997: 270) where Murdoch announces her aim 'to use certain philosophical conceptions in the diagnosis of certain literary ills'.

3. The contraction of all of philosophy to one image is of course no more amazing than the contraction of all literature to one image. However, my comments on the latter are limited, as I am not considering Murdoch's understanding of literature here, but her understanding of literature in the way in which it functions in her philosophical thought.

4. Murdoch refers to Hampshire's *Thought and Action* (1959) for a developed image of what she there describes as 'ideally rational man'. She will refer to this text again in 'The Idea of Perfection', to be discussed later.

5. These remarks make for an interesting comparison with Le Doeuff's discussion of Descartes as a philosopher who recognizes his own finitude in *Hipparchia's Choice* (see Le Doeuff 1991: 89).

6. This distinction is different from, though related to, the distinction between existentialist and mystical novels, in 'Existentialists and Mystics' (Murdoch 1997: 223ff.).

7. Conradi (2001a: 375). Conradi responds here to Bloom, who 'championed Murdoch as a religious fabulist, a writer of brilliant entertainments rather than a writer excelling at the fresh invention of personalities' (see Bloom 1986: 30–31).

8. Murdoch (1997: 261). The problem referred to consists of a literary and a moral aspect: 'Is the Liberal-democratic theory of personality an adequate one?' and 'What is characteristic of the greatest literary works of art?' or 'What, chiefly, makes Tolstoy the greatest of novelists and Shakespeare the greatest of writers?'

9. Conradi (1997: xxii). I shall be speaking here only of Sartre. He was, of course, not the only existentialist thinker nor the only one discussed by Murdoch. There is also, for example, Marcel, whose Gifford Lectures, *The Mystery of Being*, Murdoch discusses in 'The Image of the Mind' (1951). His thoughts should be much closer to Murdoch's for he, as Phillips notes, 'stresses the need for true communication with others' (Phillips 1991: 45). Phillips notices Murdoch's 'serious interest in and close knowledge of Marcel's philosophy', but she assumes that 'Marcel's thought has probably not influenced and as shaped Murdoch's own philosophical stance as deeply and as directly as Simone Weil's has' (Phillips 1991: 63 n. 1). Marcel is rarely mentioned in Murdoch's later work.

10. Whether Murdoch was ever an existentialist has been debated. Warnock 'roughly' applies the title still in *Women Philosophers* in 1996 (Warnock 1996: xliii). Conradi reproaches her for doing so, calling her claim 'doubtful and inattentive' (Conradi 1997: xxii).

11. Spear (1995: 8). The quote from *Sartre: Romantic Rationalist* is taken from Murdoch (1999: 138).

12. Murdoch says too that consciousness '*is* nothing'. This may be misleading. It should of course not be understood to imply that there is no consciousness. Rather, consciousness relates to itself and to everything else as to something it is not. This is the origin of freedom for human beings (cf. Sartre 2003).

13. Murdoch (1997: 20). Yet, in the same interview she confesses to feeling *horror* at the thought that the same verdict is applied to her own work.

14. 'The Idea of Perfection' in: *Yale Review* 53.3 (spring 1964), 342–380; *The Sovereignty of Good Over Other Concepts*, London: Cambridge University Press, 1967 (Leslie Stephen Lecture); 'On "God" and "Good"' in M. Grene (ed.), *The Anatomy of Knowledge* (London: Routledge and Kegan Paul, 1969), pp. 233–258. 'The Idea of Perfection' is based on the Ballard Matthews lecture, which Murdoch gave in 1962 at University College North Wales. 'The Sovereignty of Good Over Other Concepts' was the Leslie Stephen Lecture in 1967, held in Cambridge.

15. In 'On "God" and "Good"' Murdoch proceeds by wondering in what way prayer can still be valuable for those she calls 'unreligious believers'. Would it be possible for them to direct their attention to the Good? What would such a Good be like? In 'The Sovereignty of Good Over Other Concepts' she considers the metaphor of the Good in answer to a question she also asks in 'On "God" and "Good"': 'How can we make ourselves better?' (Murdoch 1997: 368; cf. Murdoch 1997: 342).

16. These images are present in the other two essays as well, even though the confrontation with linguistic analysis is less turbulent there. Compare the first paragraphs of 'On "God" and "Good"' and of 'The Sovereignty of Good Over Other Concepts'.

17. Cf. Murdoch 1997: 324, 340 and 359.

18. Murdoch's concern for forgotten facts recalls Woolf's challenge regarding facts about women in *A Room of One's Own*. See especially chapter three where Woolf brilliantly subverts the facts about women encountered in the British Library.

19. As Murdoch indicates herself this argument goes back to one of her earliest articles, 'Thinking and Language'.

20. The other objections she identifies as follows:

> I find the image of man which I have sketched above both alien and implausible. That is, more precisely: I have simple empirical objections (I do not think people are necessarily or essentially 'like that'), I have philosophical objections (I do not find the arguments convincing), and I have moral objections (I do not think people *ought* to picture themselves in this way). (Murdoch 1997: 306)

21. Murdoch (1997: 312). Of course, it can be disputed that religious examples are not ordinary and everyday. Again, Murdoch is not denying it is ordinary and everyday for some. It is, however, not so for the 'unreligious believers', whom she considers her prime audience.

4   Imagination

1. Murdoch merely mentions imagination in *Sartre: Romantic Rationalist* and in 'Knowing the Void' (1956), a review of Simone Weil's *Notebooks* (Murdoch 1999: 96; Murdoch 1997: 158, 159). Imagination in both texts is understood to be strictly separated from reality. And in this respect both Sartre's and Weil's notions of imagination are very different from the one Murdoch develops. She does not pursue their understandings of imagination.

2. Compare too: 'imagination . . . (good by definition) . . . fantasy (bad by definition)' (Murdoch 1993: 322).

3. The term 'mechanical' originates in Murdoch's reading of Kant. See the next part of this chapter.

4. In 'The Idea of Perfection' she expresses the difference between art and science in rather puzzling words: 'We are men and we are moral agents before we are scientists, and the place of science in human life must be discussed in *words*. This is why it is and always will be more important to know about Shakespeare than to know about any scientist: and if there is a "Shakespeare of science" his name is Aristotle' (Murdoch 1997: 326–327).

5. Compare Antonaccio's discussion of these words 'There it is' (Antonaccio 2000: 138).

6. Murdoch mentions the great but not the minor artists by name. On the latter one finds some remarks only in the interview with Magee, where she notes: 'In bad art fantasy simply take charge, as in the familiar case of the romance or thriller where the hero (alias the author) is brave, generous, indomitable, lovable (he has his faults of course) and ends the story loaded with the gifts of fortune' (Murdoch 1997: 11).

7. Of course, there are exceptions. See in particular the discussion of *King Lear* in the fifth chapter of *Metaphysics as a Guide to Morals*.

8. Wood (1999: 179 and 180 respectively); cf. Murdoch (1997: 205).

9. This line is quoted by Bronzwaer (1988: 63).

10. Note the quotation marks around that word: 'mechanically' may also refer to it being used in connection to fantasy, later on (cf. Murdoch 1993: 320).

11. Compare, for example, Kearney (1988), McMullin (1996), Strawson (1971), Warnock (1976).

12. Murdoch (1993: 316 and 308 respectively). Warnock and McMullin point out that imagination had this function also for earlier thinkers (Descartes, Locke, Berkeley, Hume). Yet, they note too that Kant gives a larger role to this notion of imagination than his predecessors. McMullin refers to *Critique of Pure Reason* A78/B103 (Warnock 1976: 13–15, 33 and McMullin 1996: 238; see also Strawson 1971).

13. The essay 'Ethics and Imagination', published five years earlier and also based on the 1982 Gifford Lectures is to a large extent identical to the chapter in *Metaphysics as a Guide to Morals*, yet it omits part of the text. The part added runs from 'Kant here connects imagination essentially with the conception of an object' on page 308 to page 309 'Kant saw that space-and-time was "a special case", to be seen as a "form of intuition"; so was morality, to be seen as a unique operation of reason'.

14. This is true too of the addition on Coleridge, later in the chapter. This part runs from the last part of the discussion of Kant, from page 315 the sentence starting with 'Kant himself does not . . .' to Virgil's advice on page 317.

15. See also Warnock (1976: 30 and 31). See Strawson (1971: 42) and Kearney (1988: 168–169 and also 427 n. 29) for a short discussion of Kant's understanding of transcendental.

16. Compare here Warnock:

> Kant held that to determine these general forms is the task of transcendental philosophy, while to determine what reminds me of a palm tree is the task of psychology. It is not entirely obvious that this is a proper distinction, but we can at least distinguish between particular psychological truths about individual people, which are part of the history of those people, and general psychological truths about people at large. What Kant is offering us is *a general psychological truth* about the function of imagination, but a truth which he claims is not only universally applicable, but can be shown to be *necessarily* true. (Warnock 1976: 31, emphasis in original)

17. This attempt she compares to earlier ones in which she argued against networks of concepts or language. Murdoch detects this network of language in the analytical philosophy she encountered in Oxford, but later also in postmodernism. In her earlier work 'The Sublime and the Beautiful Revisited', she used words like 'convention' to express the idea that humans are operated by a system they cannot change (Murdoch 1997: 217ff.; cf. Antonaccio 2000: 101–113, 180–184).

18. It is almost impossible to fully translate the venom of Nietzsche's criticism in the repetitive 'vermöge eines Vermögens' (*Beyond Good and Evil*, 11). 'By means of a means' would be closer to the German original than 'by means of a faculty'.

19. This is, incidentally, a form of writing found regularly in Murdoch. With a single remark she refers to arguments explored elsewhere, though it is hardly unrecognizable for anyone who does not know this earlier work.

20. The present discussion of Murdoch's understanding of Kant's notion of the beautiful leaves out the more familiar aspect that she does mention, as well as those she does not (like the relationship of this critique to the first two). The elements left out are, for example, the distinction between dependent and independent beauty, and the shared appreciation of art (*sensus communis*) (Murdoch 1997: 207, 212). Especially in 'The Sublime and the Good', these aspects read as a reiteration of Kant's text, rather than part of Murdoch's argument. Murdoch is most of all concerned with the sublime, and with genius.

21. Cf. Warnock (1976: 47); cf. Kant, *Critique of Judgment*, book II, section 9.

22. Note that this is only true of independent beauty.

23. Again, it is Hampshire who is regarded as representing this view (Murdoch 1997: 210–211). Compare other essays (for example, 'Against Dryness'), where Murdoch strongly opposes the notion of an object of art as isolated and on its own.

24. Cf. Murdoch (1997: 209 and 212), where a similar argument is used against Tolstoy, in a way that now seems naive. Wood complains about this form of art theory, as illogical: 'If one simply *knows* "independently" that Shakespeare is great (though Murdoch never tells us whence comes this independence: nor can she, of course), then one cannot test one's aesthetic by recourse to Shakespeare' (Wood 1999: 179ff., emphasis in original).

25. Compare Warnock (1976: 55ff.); cf. *Critique of Judgment*, book II, section 28).

26. Murdoch makes the following comparison with structuralism:

> We may compare here the place given to genius in structuralist theory, where the original creative artist, philosopher, scientist, as inventor of language and meaning, is exempt from the general conventional preformed linguistic rules or codes whereby 'language speaks the man'. Structuralism, sometimes offered as 'scientific', is in its general tendency an aesthetic system of value. (1993: 313)

27. Compare 'On "God" and "Good" ', where Murdoch suggests that one may try to 'incarnate' perfection by wanting to write like Shakespeare, or to paint like Piero della Fransesca. 'But of course one knows that Shakespeare and Piero, though almost like gods, are not gods, and that one has got to do the thing oneself alone and differently' (Murdoch 1997: 350–351).

28. For the quotation of Kant, Murdoch refers to the *Critique of Judgment*, book II, Analytic of the Sublime, section 53.

29. The superfluous quotation marks around imagination seem to emphasize the difference between Murdoch's and the Romantic understanding of imagination. I suspect that Murdoch would have used a different word if she could have.

30. In the past twenty to thirty years the interest in imagination has occasioned several books on the topic. Some of these are mentioned in the footnotes throughout this chapter. Others can be found in the bibliography.

31. The similarity between Murdoch and Romantic thinkers has occasionally been suggested to me, but until very recently I had not found any reference to it in the secondary literature. Unfortunately, it has not been possible to consider Laverty (2007) here, who argues that philosophical Romanticism provides a unique way

of presenting the distinctive elements in Murdoch's philosophy (Laverty 2007: 3).
My subsequent discussion only considers the difference Murdoch notes between her
understanding of imagination and that of the Romantics. It will simply accept
Murdoch's reasons for bypassing the Romantic notion of imagination.

32. See also Murdoch (1997: 235): 'The Romantics felt instinctively that science was
an enemy of art, and of course in certain simple and obvious ways they were right.'

33. Cf.: 'The great Romantics ... transcended "Romanticism" (1997: 369). Cf. too
Murdoch (1997: 261): 'The word "Romantic" is best defined by what it is opposed
to' In this essay one finds the most extensive discussion of the Romantic
movement.

34. In these characteristics the Romantic Movement is certainly different from the
acclaimed nineteenth-century novel (see Murdoch 1997: 271).

35. Murdoch (1999: 111): 'When in insuperable practical difficulties a sense of
"all or nothing" is what *consoles*. ... The general impression of Sartre's work is certainly that of a powerful but abstract model of a hopeless dilemma, coloured by a
surreptitious romanticism which embraces the hopelessness.' Cf. too Murdoch
(1997: 223): 'The existentialist novel is the natural heir and outcome of the Western
nineteenth-century thought and is the child of the Romantic movement.'

36. Perhaps Murdoch's account of the Romantic notion of imagination indicates the
extent of her knowledge of Coleridge or Wordsworth. In her various overviews
Coleridge is mentioned only occasionally and Wordsworth not at all. She may
have accepted contemporary prejudices, where Coleridge is not considered a philosopher or even an original thinker. Warnock's chapters on Coleridge are in
this respect revealing in their attempt to handle the unsystematic nature of his
thought and writings (see Warnock 1976: chapter three). See too Jasper: 'Norman
Frumann's *Coleridge: The Damaged Archangel* (1972) stands as a sad monument to the
tendency of many critics to regard Coleridge's work as little more than a mosaic
drawn from his extraordinary wide reading. The danger is, then, that he becomes
merely a channel for the work and ideas of others ...' (Note how a similar danger
threatens any study of Murdoch's philosophical work.) Jasper's study intends to
counter this image and argue that Coleridge is 'a unique genius who was yet
highly sensitive and original in his reading' (Jasper 1985: 8). Perhaps too Murdoch
regards her disapproval of the deification of art as more important than any possible agreement.

37. This Greek word 'phantasia' may be the source for Murdoch's own use of
fantasy. Murdoch does not reveal the origin of her use of the term. The closest she
comes to etymology is when she states that the distinction between imagination
and fantasy is not the same as Coleridge's distinction between imagination and
fancy (Murdoch 1993: 321).

38. 'One might take the *Republic* (597) passage about the painter as indicating art
which was bad because thoughtless' (Murdoch 1993: 317).

39. See too page 392 for a discussion of *Ion*, in which Socrates smirks at Ion for
his ignorance of anything but the art of recitation, and page 416 for a discussion
of the *Phaedrus*. Cf. too Murdoch (1993: 317): 'Plato refers more than once to the

unconscious non-rational creativity of poets who do not know how they do it and
cannot explain what they have done. That great artist had mixed feelings about
such dangerous gifts.'

40. See respectively Murdoch (1997: 158, 341 and 364).

41. Compare here Murdoch (1997: 443): 'St John of the Cross says that God is the
abyss of faith into which we fall when we have discarded all images of him. This is
the point at which Plato starts making jokes.' Cf. Murdoch (1993: 320):

> The spiritual life is a long disciplined destruction of false images and false goods
> until (in some sense which we cannot understand) the imagining mind achieves
> an end of images and shadows (*ex umbris et imaginibus in veritatem*), the final *demytho-
> logisation* of the religious passion as expressed by mystics such as Eckhart and
> St. John of the Cross.

42. Murdoch points to the image of God as a creative artist at the end of *The Sophist* as
well as in the *Timaeus* (Murdoch 1993: 319–320).

5   Morality, Religion and the Ontological Proof

1. Cf. Murdoch (1993: 318): 'It is very difficult to understand "what goes on" in the
souls of dedicated religious people, even when we know them face to face and they
are trying to tell us. It is also difficult to *imagine* ways of life which are much above
our own moral level as being morally demanded. They exert no magnetism and
cannot be seen except in terms of senseless deprivation.' (Emphasis in original)

2. Religions are generally understood to consist of more than belief in God or Good, or
to be not just a sustainer of morality. Murdoch here differs significantly from discussions of actual religions. See, for example, Smart, who distinguishes the following aspects: practical and ritual dimension, experiential and emotional dimension,
narrative or mythic dimension, doctrinal and philosophical dimension, ethical and
legal dimension, social and institutional dimension, material dimension (Smart
1998: 12–21).

3. Compare Murdoch (1997: 443). In her reviews of both *Acastos* and of *The Fire and the
Sun* Nussbaum starts by relating her expectations, only to find these disappointed.
This returning structure makes one wonder whether Murdoch is fully to blame for
these disappointments.

4. Or, does Socrates talk in jest?

> SOCRATES: I think we've passed beyond the gods. No one seems to want to defend
> them except me.
> TIMONAX: Socrates!
> ALCIBIADES: He's a deep one. We don't know how to have him! (Murdoch
> 1997: 522)

5. Despite the stage setting as 'Athens in the late fifth century BC' (Murdoch
1997: 496), the dialogue is both contemporary and historical. This is suggested

by the author's note that the piece is to be performed either in modern dress or in period costume (Murdoch 1997: 527).

6. Compare, for instance, Clack and Clack (1998: 6). Clack and Clack discuss here how many works suggest that theism is the main concern of the philosophy of religion (see Clack and Clack 1998: 190 n. 11 and 191 n. 12 for references). In this book Clack and Clack offer alternative approaches as well. Note also that Murdoch has been called 'a friend to theistic religion' (Gamwell 1996: 175; cf. Schweiker 1996: 209), because her interest in religious ideas is exceptional among contemporary philosophers. The phrase 'god of the philosophers' was the first line on a piece of paper found sewn into Pascal's coat after his death, relating what he experienced one night in 1654.

7. Cf. Kerr on what he calls the general misconception of religion, in particular Christianity, by philosophers (Kerr 1997: viiff.; compare the discussions of the various authors, and in particular page 154).

8. It is in this context revealing to consider three essays by theologians in Antonaccio and Schweiker's *Iris Murdoch and the Search for Human Goodness* (1996). All three consider Murdoch's moral philosophy and its limits for a Christian (theistic) position. That is, as (confessed) Christian theologians they embraced Murdoch's work (especially Hauerwas openly confesses to having done so) at least partly because she is one of the few philosophers who take religion seriously. Yet, they now find they need to reconsider their initial enthusiasms, because Murdoch's thoughts are not as hospitable for Christianity as first assumed (see Gamwell 1996: 171–189; Hauerwas 1996: 190–208; Schweiker 1996: 209–235).

9. Compare also Murdoch (1993: 416).

10. Tracy even argues that *Metaphysics as a Guide to Morals* ' – even more than Murdoch's explicitly Platonic dialogues in *Acastos* – seems to me more faithful to the kind of form needed for rendering a Platonic theory of the Good in the late twentieth century . . . For *Metaphysics as a Guide to Morals*, in spite of its occasional appearance of meandering formlessness, seems less a treatise and more like the great mime-like Platonic dialogues' (Tracy 1996: 66).

11. Reading Plato's dialogues *as* dialogues is not common practice. For example, the main speaker in *The Sophist* has been regarded as Plato's spokesperson, even when he is called a stranger rather than guest from Elea (xenos), and even though he commits parricide by arguing that 'non-being is'. For readings that do regard the dramatic aspects of the dialogue see, for instance, Rosen (1983). See also Sallis (1986) for a general discussion on reading Platonic dialogues. Rosen is not surprisingly quoted with approval in *Metaphysics as a Guide to Morals* for another observation on Plato: 'Stanley Rosen, in his excellent book *The Quarrel between Philosophy and Poetry*, speaking of Heidegger's failure to understand Plato, suggests that the elusive Being which Heidegger attempts to discover for us is in fact the *light* which illuminates the atmosphere of the Platonic dialogues' (Murdoch 1993: 142).

12. When contemplating the Good the characters in Plato's dialogues also employ imagery, most famously the allegory of the cave, where the sun represents the Good.

Murdoch considers this imagery at length in 'The Sovereignty of Good Over Other Concepts' and *The Fire and the Sun* in particular.

13. In Plato's dialogues Plato and Socrates never appear together, which explains perhaps why it is such a fertile ground for other writers' imagination (cf., for instance, Scruton 1998). There are only three references to Plato in Plato's own dialogues (*Apology* 34a, 38b and *Phaedo* 59b). Socrates appears of course in most of Plato's dialogues and Alcibiades only in *The Symposium*. The names of the other three characters are not taken from Plato's dialogues, but from Greek mythology. The characters in 'Above the Gods' are almost the opposite of their namesakes. Acastos is son of Peleus, Antagoras a poet, Timonax a king.

14. See respectively Murdoch (1997: 498, 500, 502, 505), and Murdoch (1997: 509, 513).

15. Murdoch (1978: 179), where Charles notes that 'James and the fly looked at each other'.

16. It is a reminder of Murdoch's great admiration for Wittgenstein. Compare: 'SOCRATES: Beware in philosophy of things which 'must be so', at least look at them with a cool eye' (Murdoch, Above the Gods, p. 524) and: 'And of course, as Wittgenstein pointed out, the fact that one is irresistibly impelled to say it need not mean that anything *else* is the case' (Murdoch 1997: 316; Wittgenstein, *Philosophical Investigations*, nr. 299).

17. See *Apology* 38a, and Murdoch (1997: 299–300) respectively.

18. See Conradi (2001a: 108–109, 314, 392 n. 13) for references to *The Sacred and Profane Love Machine*, *The Sea, The Sea, Nuns and Soldiers* and *The Philosopher's Pupil*.

19. This too is very important in Antonaccio's reading of the proof. She argues that for Murdoch the proof starts in consciousness (Antonaccio 2000: chapters five and six).

20. Steel provides the references in both texts. The Seneca text is found in his *quaestiones naturales*, I, 13, 7s: 'Quid est deus? ... Sic demum magnitudo illi sua redditur, qua nulla maius cogitari potest, ...'; Augustine's in *De libero arbitrio*, II, VI, 14, where Augustine considers God's existence proven with the demonstration of the existence of a being 'quo nullus est superior' (Anselmus 1981: 50 n. 19). Please note: Steel provides an extensive commentary to Anselm's *Proslogion* in Anselmus (1981), which has Anselm's text on the right page and Steel's notes on the left, as well as an introduction. According to the convention used in this book, I refer to this text as Anselmus (1981). I have used Steel's translation, as well as Anselm (1974), which is the same translation as the one Murdoch uses.

21. The quotation is taken from P. Tillich, *Systematic Theology*, Part I, section I.

22. The list is Steel's (Anselmus 1981: 7; cf. 26). Compare too pages 7–8, where (like Murdoch) Steel seems to suggest that the proof is for thinkers (plural) rather than for the individual believer: 'Deze tekst zal dus een zeer gevarieerd publiek kunnen interesseren: theologen en filosofen, metafysici, logici, taalfilosofen, mediaevisten en – waarom niet? – de gelovige "die zoekt naar inzicht in zijn geloof".' [This text may interest a very diverse audience: theologians and philosophers, metaphysicians, logicians, philosophers of language, mediaevalists and – why not? –

the believer who 'seeks to understand his faith'.] For extensive overviews of scholarship on Anselm's proof, see Steel's introduction (Anselmus 1981: 9–31), McGill (1968: 33–110).

23. Steel refers to F. Schmitt, *Anselm von Canterbury* (Stuttgart/Bad Cannstadt, 1962) as one who favours a typically rationalistic interpretation of the ontological proof and who considers this first chapter as literary ornamentation. Steel mentions in contrast two articles by A. Stolz, which give a more significant role to this chapter. Thinking is happening in speaking to God (pros-logion). See A. Stolz, 'Zur Theologie Anselms im Proslogion' (*Catholica* 2 (1933), pp. 1–24) and A. Stolz, 'Das Proslogion des Hl. Anselms' (*Revue Bénédictine* 47 (1935), pp. 331–347). See Steel too on the division of the remaining chapters (Anselmus 1981: 22–23 and 40 n. 10). Murdoch follows Stolz's classical division.

24. Cf. Steel, who also remarks that it may not be correct to consider the argument as a syllogism. Anselm is concerned with one argument (*unum argumentum*). What is proven is the same as the proof itself (Anselmus 1981: 48–50 n. 19; see also n. 24 for the understanding of the argument as *reductio ad absurdum*).

25. See also Steel's comments (Anselmus 1981: 52 n. 25). Note too that Kant did not direct his criticism at Anselm directly, for he did not know his work, as Steel points out (Anselmus 1981: 26).

26. See also Antonaccio (2000: 125). Cf. 214 n. 28 where Antonaccio remarks that '[t]his line of interpretation has been pursued by Charles Hartshorne and Norman Malcolm'. Steel also refers to Hartshorne and Malcolm (Anselmus 1981: 54 n. 26), but considers Karl Barth's *Fides quaerens intellectum* (1931) to be the first to make a distinction between the two chapters.

27. Compare also Taylor (1996), in particular pages 18–28.

28. Steel considers it remarkable that Anselm first directs his answer to the Christian and not to the fool, but also notes that later in his answer Anselm will show that even a non-believer can understand that than which nothing greater can be thought (Anselmus 1981: 140 n. 117). Compare too nn. 149 and 145, where Steel notes the difference between talking of God and talking of that than which nothing greater can be thought. God can only be understood by believers, that than which nothing greater can be thought by all.

29. See also Steel's comments (Anselmus 1981: 162 n. 147).

30. Steel remarks that when encountering a contradiction Anselm often looks for a solution by means of a semantic analysis. Another example is found in chapter VIII, concerning the assertion: God can (not) do everything (Anselmus 1981: 56 n. 31).

31. Compare Steel's comments (Anselmus 1981: 128–129 n. 104).

32. This is argued, for instance, by Hayen (another orthodox Christian). See Hayen (1968).

33. Hayen is quoting from P. Vignaux, *Philosophy in the Middle Ages*, translated by E.C. Hall (New York: Meridian, 1959), 39ff. Vignaux remarks on the first chapter of the *Proslogion*: 'It is a dialogue of the creature with his Creator: *quaero vultum tuum*, "I seek your face." This desire to see the face of God lies in a creature –

in ourselves – who have been created precisely for that vision. Nevertheless, we
have never done that for which we were made.'

34.   Hayen (1968: 168ff.):

> ... it is a matter of participating in the redemptive work of the first born from the
> dead, of entering into the struggle of Christ against the devil, into the victory
> achieved by Jesus, who must continue to reign 'until he has placed all his enemies
> under the feet, so that God may be everything to everyone' (I Cor. 15: 25, 28),
> which is to say, so that God may be everything in the reason of the fool, just as he
> is everything in the mind of Anselm and the monks, and in that of the blessed who
> already contemplate the Father face to face.

35.   Compare McGill (1968: 63), who argues that Hayden is one of the

> [s]everal Frenchspeaking Roman Catholics scholars [who] insist on the impor-
> tance of faith, but question Barth's further thesis about Anselm and the fool.
> How, they ask, can Barth say that Anselm constantly sets himself 'against' the
> fool, that he refuses to have anything to do with him in his belief and only 'lets
> him go on repeating his counterthesis until the last day'? (Cf. Hayen 1968: 168
> as well as n. 30)

36.   'And come thou now, O Lord my God, teach my heart where and how it may seek
thee, where and how it may find thee. Lord, if thou art not here, where shall I seek
thee, being absent? But if thou art everywhere, why do I not see thee present?'
(Anselm 1974: 3).

37.   I noted before how she introduces 'individuals' into her text who question the argument. In 'On "God" and "Good"' she even admits to being 'often more than half
persuaded to think in these terms myself' (Murdoch 1997: 359). The regular use of
'we', too, includes both her readers and herself.

38.   Quotation from *Mauvaises Pensées et Autres*, Pléiade edition, vol. II, 785.

39.   'God exists, but he is out of reach. . . . As a result the nineteenth and twentieth centuries seem to many writers a time when God is no more present . . . and not yet
again present . . . In this time of the no longer and not yet, man is "Wandering
between two worlds, one dead,/The other powerless to be born".' (Hillis Miller
1963: 1–2); the quotation is taken from C.B. Tinker and H.F. Lowry (eds), *The Poe-
tical Works of Matthew Arnold* (London, 1950, 302).

Coda: Women and Philosophy

1.   Woolf is even more subject to such dismissal, and surrounded by various myths: she
was a snob, anti-Semitic, anorectic, mad, etc. Lee very perceptively discusses these
claims throughout her biography (Lee 1997: *passim*).

2.   In the reception of her work, it has not always been appreciated that Woolf meant
'common' to mean 'general or ordinary', rather than 'vulgar'. Lee argues that

Woolf is partly to blame here, as she used to refer to the common reader as 'he' in her desire to avoid exposure (Lee 1997: 414–415).

3. This is a quick answer. A much longer answer can be found in Le Doeuff's *The Sex of Knowing*.

4. Midgley notes in her memoirs that while it is understandable that so much attention has been given to Murdoch's last years, when she was ill with Alzheimer's, it is also regrettable: 'unfortunately, the workings of the publicity machine see to it that people are usually remembered for only one thing. And to be remembered only – or even primarily – for the disease that destroyed one is surely a horrid misfortune, an especially unsuitable fate for someone the rest of whose life was as full and active as hers was' (Midgley 2005: 85–86).

5. Warnock (2000: 39). This is how Warnock explains how Foot, Anscombe and Murdoch all became 'remarkable and original women' (cf. Chapter 2).

6. Descartes would probably agree here. Yet, he would not consider common sense a good starting point for philosophy.

7. There is always the question whether I have defended Murdoch too much. The frequent use of 'simple' and 'surely' would not be accepted in an undergraduate essay, as a respondent once pointed out. These doubts will always linger, but I believe it is important to read a philosopher on his or her own terms, and to stay with their thoughts as long as possible. Moreover, Murdoch was keenly aware of the limitations of her philosophical writing. The harsh references to her philosophical works in her novels are not just expressions of the dissatisfaction that many authors feel when finishing a book, but often perceptive criticisms.

8. Think here for example of the rewritten history in *A Room of One's Own*.

9. Compare here too Rowe: 'In *Women in the House of Fiction*, Lorna Sage notes that like Elizabeth Gaskell and George Eliot, "Murdoch puts the woman question to one side" ... Exploring the very considerable connection between Eliot and Murdoch, however, waits for another essay' (Rowe 2004: 93 n. 2).

Bibliography

Works by Murdoch

Philosophy

Sartre: Romantic Rationalist. London: Vintage, 1999 (1953).

The Sovereignty of Good. London and New York: Routledge Classics, 2001 (1970).

The Fire and the Sun: Why Plato Banished the Artist. Oxford: Clarendon Press, 1977.

[untitled]. *PR Review* 13 no. 6.5 (1979), p. 5.

Acastos: Two Platonic Dialogues. New York: Viking Penguin, 1986.

'Hoe bewijs ik het bestaan van God: Enkele bespiegelingen omtrent het ontologisch bewijs', translation R. Verhoef. *De Volkskrant*, 1986.

'Ethics and Imagination'. *Irish Theological Quarterly* 52.1–2 (1986), 81–95.

Metaphysics as a Guide to Morals. London: Penguin Books, 1993 (1992).

Existentialists and Mystics: Writings on Philosophy and Literature. London: Chatto and Windus, 1997.

Novels

Under the Net. London: Chatto and Windus, 1954.

The Flight from the Enchanter. London: Chatto and Windus, 1956.

The Sandcastle. London: Chatto and Windus, 1957.

The Bell. London: Chatto and Windus, 1958.

A Severed Head. London: Chatto and Windus, 1961.

An Unofficial Rose. London: Chatto and Windus, 1962.

The Unicorn. London: Chatto and Windus, 1963.

The Italian Girl. London: Chatto and Windus, 1964.

The Red and the Green. London: Chatto and Windus, 1965.

The Time of the Angels. London: Chatto and Windus, 1966.

The Nice and the Good. London: Chatto and Windus, 1968.

Bruno's Dream. London: Chatto and Windus, 1969.

A Fairly Honourable Defeat. London: Chatto and Windus, 1970.

An Accidental Man. London: Chatto and Windus, 1971.

The Black Prince. London: Chatto and Windus, 1973.

The Sacred and Profane Love Machine. London: Chatto and Windus, 1974.

A Word Child. London: Chatto and Windus, 1975.

Henry and Cato. London: Chatto and Windus, 1976.

The Sea, The Sea. London: Chatto and Windus, 1978.

Nuns and Soldiers. London: Chatto and Windus, 1980.

The Philosopher's Pupil. London: Chatto and Windus, 1983.

The Good Apprentice. London: Chatto and Windus, 1985.

The Book and the Brotherhood. London: Chatto and Windus, 1987.

The Message to the Planet. London: Chatto and Windus, 1989.

The Green Knight. London: Chatto and Windus, 1993.

Jackson's Dilemma. London: Chatto and Windus, 1995.

Critical Commentary

Monographs and Edited Collections

Antonaccio, M. (2000). *Picturing the Human: The Moral Thought of Iris Murdoch*. Oxford: Oxford University Press.

Antonaccio, M. and W. Schweiker (eds) (1996). *Iris Murdoch and the Search for Human Goodness*. Chicago and London: The University of Chicago Press.

Backus, G. (1986). *Iris Murdoch: The Novelist as Philosopher, the Philosopher as Novelist: 'The Unicorn' as a Philosophical Novel*. Bern: P. Lang.

Bayley, J. (1998). *Iris: A Memoir of Iris Murdoch*. London: Duckworth.

Bayley, J. (1999). *Iris and the Friends*. London: Duckworth.

Byatt, A.S. (1994). *Degrees of Freedom: The Early Novels of Iris Murdoch*. London: Vintage.

Chevalier, J.-L. (ed.) (1978). *Recontres avec Iris Murdoch*. Centre de Recherches de Littérature et Linguistique des Pays de Langue Anglaise, l'Université de Caen.

Conradi, P. (2001a). *The Saint and the Artist: A Study of the Fiction of Iris Murdoch*. London: HarperCollins.

Conradi, P. (2001b). *Iris Murdoch: A Life*. London: HarperCollins.

Dipple, E. (1982). *Iris Murdoch: Work for the Spirit*. London: Methuen.

Dooley, G. (ed.) (2003). *From a Tiny Corner in the House of Fiction: Conversations with Iris Murdoch*. Columbia: University of South Carolina Press.

Fletcher, J., and C. Bove (1994). *Iris Murdoch: A Descriptive Primary and Annotated Secondary Bibliography*. New York: Garland.

Goldberg, S. (1993). *Agents and Lives: Moral Thinking in Literature*. Cambridge: Cambridge University Press.

Gordon, D.J. (1995). *Iris Murdoch's Fables of Unselfing*. Columbia and London: University of Missouri Press.

Griffin, G. (1993). *The Influence of the Writings of Simone Weil on the Fiction of Iris Murdoch*. San Francisco: Mellen University Press.

Grimshaw, T. (2005). *Sexuality, Gender, and Power in Iris Murdoch's Fiction*. Madison, Taeneck: Fairleigh Dickinson University Press.

Hawkins, P.S. (1993). *The Language of Grace: Flannery O' Connor, Walker Percy and Iris Murdoch*. Cambridge, MA: Cowley Publications.

Jansen, H. (2001). *Laughter Among the Ruins: Postmodern Comic Approaches to Suffering*. Frankfurt am Main: Peter Lang Verlag.

Johnson, D. (1987). *Iris Murdoch*. Brighton: The Harvester Press.

Kerr, F. (1997). *Immortal Longings: Versions of Transcending Humanity*. London: SPCK.

Laverty, M. (2007). *Iris Murdoch's Ethics: A Consideration of her Romantic Vision*. London, New York: Continuum.

O'Connell, P. (1996). *To Love the Good: The Moral Philosophy of Iris Murdoch*. New York: Peter Lang.

Phillips, D. (1991). *Agencies of the Good in Iris Murdoch*. Frankfurt am Main, New York: Peter Lang.

Ramanathan, S. (1990). *Iris Murdoch: Figures of Good*. Houndsmills, Basingstoke, London: Macmillan Press.

Rowe, A. (ed.) (2006). *Iris Murdoch: A Reassessment*. Houndsmills, Basingstoke: Palgrave Macmillan.

Seiler-Franklin, C. (1979). *Boulder-Pushers: Women in the Fiction of Margaret Drabble, Doris Lessing and Iris Murdoch*. Bern: Lang.

Spear, H. (1995). *Iris Murdoch*. Basingstoke: Macmillan.

Todd, R. (ed.) (1988). *Encounters with Iris Murdoch*. Amsterdam: Free University Press.

Turner, J. (1993). *Murdoch vs. Freud: A Freudian Look at an Anti-Freudian*. New York: Lang.

Widdows, H. (2005). *The Moral Vision of Iris Murdoch*. Aldershot: Ashgate.

Reviews and Articles

Allen, D. (1974). 'Two Experiences of Existence: Jean-Paul Sartre and Iris Murdoch'. *International Philosophical Quarterly* 14.2 (June), 181–187.

Altorf, M. (2006). 'Reassessing Iris Murdoch in the Light of Feminist Philosophy: Michèle Le Doeuff and the Philosophical Imaginary'. In A. Rowe (ed.), *Iris Murdoch: A Reassessment*. Houndsmills, Basingstoke: Palgrave Macmillan, pp. 175–186.

Altorf, M., and M. Willemsen (2003). 'Iris Murdoch en de verbeelding van het Goede'. I. Murdoch, *Over God en het Goede*. Translated and introduced by M. Altorf and M. Willemsen. Amsterdam: Boom, pp. 7–30.

Antonaccio, M. (1994). [Review of *Metaphysics as a Guide to Morals*]. *Journal of Religion* 74.2, 278–280.

Antonaccio, M. (1996). 'Form and Contingency in Iris Murdoch's Ethics'. In M. Antonaccio and W. Schweiker (eds), *Iris Murdoch and the Search for Human Goodness*. Chicago and London: The University of Chicago Press, pp. 110–137.

Bloom, H. (1986). 'A Comedy of Worldly Salvation'. *New York Times Book Review*, 12 January, 30–31.

Bronzwaer, W. (1988). 'Images of Plato in "The Fire and the Sun" and "Acastos"'. In R. Todd (ed.), *Encounters with Iris Murdoch*. Amsterdam: Free University Press, pp. 55–67.

Brugmans, E. (2001). 'Iris Murdoch en de soevereiniteit van het goede'. *De Uil van Minerva* 17.4, 213–223.

Brugmans, E. (2004). 'Fundamenten en methoden in Murdochs moraalfilosofie'. *Tijdschrift voor Filosofie* 66.1, 3–29.

Cohan, S. (1982). 'From Subtext to Dream Text: The Brutal Egoism of Iris Murdoch's Male Narrators'. *Women and Literature* 2, 222–242.

Conradi, P. (1997). 'Editor's Preface'. In I. Murdoch, *Existentialists and Mystics: Writings on Philosophy and Literature*. London: Chatto and Windus, pp. xix–xxx.

Conradi, P. (2001c). 'Did Iris Murdoch Draw from Life?'. *Iris Murdoch News Letter* 15 (winter), 4–7.

Diamond, C. (1996). ' "We Are Perpetually Moralists": Iris Murdoch, Fact, and Value'. In M. Antonaccio and W. Schweiker (eds), *Iris Murdoch and the Search for Human Goodness*. Chicago and London: The University of Chicago Press, pp. 79–109.

Gamwell, F.I. (1996). 'On the Loss of Theism'. In M. Antonaccio and W. Schweiker (eds), *Iris Murdoch and the Search for Human Goodness*. Chicago and London: The University of Chicago Press, pp. 171–189.

Goshgarian, G. (1972). 'Feminist Values in the Novels of Iris Murdoch'. *Revue des Langues Vivantes* 40, 519–527.

Haasse, H. (1965). ' "Dreadfully significant": Over het werk van Iris Murdoch'. *Leestekens*. Amsterdam: Querido, pp. 95–111.

Hacking, I. (1992). 'Plato's Friend'. *London Review of Books*, 17 December, 8–9.

Hauerwas, S. (1996). 'Murdochian Muddles: Can We Get Through Them If God Does Not Exist?'. In M. Antonaccio and W. Schweiker (eds), *Iris Murdoch and the Search for Human Goodness*. Chicago and London: The University of Chicago Press, pp. 190–209.

Jasper, D. (1986). ' "And after Art, . . . nothing": Iris Murdoch and the possibility of a metaphysic'. *Universities Quarterly: Culture, Education & Society* 40.2 (Winter), 137–146.

Lievers, M. (2001). [review of Conradi's *A Life*]. *NRC Handelsblad*, 19 October.

Loades, A. (1999). [review of M. Antonaccio, W. Schweiker (eds), *Iris Murdoch and the Search for Human Goodness*]. *Literature and Theology* 13.1, 94–95.

Mason, R. (1996). 'Iris Murdoch'. In S. Brown, D. Collinson and R. Wilkinson (eds), *Biographical Dictionary of Twentieth Century Philosophers*. London: Routledge, pp. 554–555.

Nicol, B. (2006). 'The Curse of *The Bell*: The Ethics and Aesthetics of Narrative'. In A. Rowe (ed.), *Iris Murdoch: A Reassessment*. Houndsmills, Basingstoke: Palgrave Macmillan, pp. 100–111.

Nussbaum, M.C. (1986a). 'Miscast in Dialogue Form'. *Times Literary Supplement* 4350 (15 August), 881.

Nussbaum, M.C. (1996). 'Love and Vision: Iris Murdoch on Eros and the Individual'. In M. Antonaccio and W. Schweiker (eds), *Iris Murdoch and the Search for Human Goodness*. Chicago and London: The University of Chicago Press, pp. 29–53.

Phillips, D. (1994/5). 'Iris Murdochs zoektocht naar het goede: de verrijkende wederzijdse beïnvloeding van scheppende verbeeldingskracht en analytisch denken'. *Wijsgerig Perspectief* 35–33, 72–77.

Ricks, Ch. (1965). 'A Sort of Mystery Novel'. *New Statesman* 22 October, 604–605.

Rowe, M. M. (2004). 'Iris Murdoch and the Case of "Too Many Men" '. *Studies in the Novel* 36-1 (Spring), 79–94.

Schweiker, W. (1996). 'The Sovereignty of God's Goodness'. In M. Antonaccio and W. Schweiker (eds), *Iris Murdoch and the Search for Human Goodness*. Chicago and London: The University of Chicago Press, pp. 209–235.

Taylor, Ch. (1996). 'Iris Murdoch and Moral Philosophy'. In M. Antonaccio and W. Schweiker (eds), *Iris Murdoch and the Search for Human Goodness*. Chicago and London: The University of Chicago Press, pp. 3–28.

Todd, R. (1994/5). 'Iris Murdoch: veertig jaar romanschrijven'. *Wijsgerig Perspectief* 35–33, 66–71.

Tracy, D. (1996). 'Iris Murdoch and the Many Faces of Platonism'. In M. Antonaccio and W. Schweiker (eds), *Iris Murdoch and the Search for Human Goodness*. Chicago and London: The University of Chicago Press, pp. 54–75.

Warnock, G.J. (1971). 'The Moralists: Value and Choices'. *Encounter* 36 (April), 81–84.

Willemsen, M.F. (1998). ' "We are simply here": Over de metafysica van Iris Murdoch'. In M. Hoenen (ed.), *Metamorphosen: Acten van de 20e Nederlands-Vlaamse Filosofiedag*. Katholieke Universiteit Nijmegen, pp. 101–114.

Wood, J. (1999). 'Iris Murdoch's Philosophy of Fiction'. *The Broken Estate: Essays on Literature and Belief*. London: Jonathan Cape, pp. 174–185.

Other Works Consulted

Alcoff, L.M. (1995–1996). 'Is the Feminist Critique of Reason Rational?' *Philosophic Exchange* 26, 59–79.

Anderson, P.S. (1998). *A Feminist Philosophy of Religion: The Rationality and Myths of Religious Belief*. Oxford: Blackwell.

Anselm of Canterbury (1974). *Basic Writings: Proslogium, Monologium, Gaunilo's: On Behalf of the Fool, Cure Deus Homo*. Translated by S.W. Deane, with an introduction by Ch. Hartshorne. La Salle, Illinois: Open Court Publishing Company.

Anselmus van Canterbury (1981). *Proslogion gevolgd door de discussie met Gaunilo*. Introduced, translated and annotated by C. Steel. Bussum: Het Wereldvenster.

Arens, K. (1995). 'Between Hypatia and Beauvoir: Philosophy as Discourse'. *Hypatia* 10–4, 46–75.

Ayer, A.J. (1936). *Language, Truth and Logic*. London: Gollancz.

Bassett, L. (2000). 'Blind Spots and Deafness'. In M. Deutscher (ed.), *Michèle Le Doeuff: Operative Philosophy and Imaginary Practice*. New York: Humanity Books, pp. 105–125.

Baumeister, Th. (1999). *De filosofie en de kunsten: van Plato tot Beuys*. Best: Damon.

Bayley, J. (1960). *The Characters of Love: A Study in the Literature of Personality*. London: Constable.

Berger, H. (1997). *Leeswijzer bij de Kritiek van de oordeelskracht*. Tilburg: Tilburg University Press.

Bergonzi, B. (1979). *The Situation of the Novel*. London and Basingstoke: Macmillan.

Brann, E.T.H. (1991). *The World of the Imagination: Sum and Substance*. Boston: Rowman & Littlefield Publishers, Inc.

Clack, B. (1997). [review of M. Warnock, *Women Philosophers*]. *Women Studies International Forum* 5–6, 452–453.

Clack, B., and B.R. Clack (1998). *The Philosophy of Religion: A Critical Introduction*. Cambridge: Polity Press.

Cocking, J.M. (1991). *Imagination: A Study in the History of Ideas*. Edited and with an introduction by P. Murray. London: Routledge.

Dante Alighieri (1996). *Divina Comedia*. Edited and translated by R.M. Durling. New York, Oxford: Oxford University Press.

De Beauvoir, S. (1997). *The Second Sex*. Translated and edited by H.M. Parshley. London: Vintage.

Deutscher, M. (ed.) (2000). *Michèle Le Doeuff: Operative Philosophy and Imaginary Practice*. New York: Humanity Books.

Deutscher, P. (2000). 'Interview: Michèle Le Doeuff, interviewed by Penelope Deutscher'. *Hypatia* 154, 236–242.

Dhanda, M., and P.S. Anderson (2002). 'Bringing Us Into Twenty-First Century Feminism with Joy and Wit: An Interview with Michèle Le Doeuff'. *Women's Philosophy Review* no. 30, 8–39.

Diogenes Laërtius (1925). *Lives and Opinions of Eminent Philosophers*. Translated by R.D. Hicks. London: Heinemann and Cambridge, Massachusetts: Harvard University Press.

Eaglestone, R. (1997). *Ethical Criticism: Reading After Levinas*. Edinburgh: Edinburgh University Press.

Engel, P. (1987). 'Continental Insularity: Contemporary French Analytical Philosophy'. In Phillips Griffiths (ed.), *Contemporary French Philosophy*. Cambridge: Cambridge University Press, pp. 1–19.

Gonzales Arnal, S. (1998). [review of M. Warnock, *Women Philosophers*]. *British Journal for the History of Philosophy*, 6–2, 306–307.

Gordon, C. (1989). 'Translator's Note'. In M. Le Doeuff, *The Philosophical Imaginary*. London: The Athlone Press, pp. vii–x.

Grosz, E. (1989). *Sexual Subversions: Three French Feminists*. Sydney: Allen & Unwin.

Hager, A. (1998). 'Lear's Fool'. In V.K. Janik (ed.), *Fools and Jesters in Literature, Art, and History: A Bio-Bibliographical Sourcebook*. Westport, Connecticut: Greenwood Press, pp. 289–297.

Hampshire, S. (1959). *Thought and Action*. London: Chatto and Windus.

Hampshire, S. (1972). 'Disposition and Memory'. *Freedom of Mind and Other Essays*. Oxford: Clarendon Press, pp. 160–182.

Hayen, A. (1968). 'The Role of the Fool in St. Anselm and the Necessarily Apostolic Character of True Christian Reflection'. In J. Hick and A.C. McGill (eds), *The Many-Faced Argument: Recent Studies on the Ontological Argument for the Existence of God*. London and Melbourne: Macmillan, pp. 162–182.

Hillis Miller, J. (1963). *The Disappearance of God: Five Nineteenth-Century Writers*. Cambridge, Massachusetts: The Belknap Press of Harvard University Press.

Hillis Miller, J. (1968). *The Forms of Victorian Fiction: Thackeray, Dickens, Trollope, George Eliot, Meredith and Hardy*. Notre Dame, London: University of Notre Dame Press.

Janik, V.K. (ed.) (1998). *Fools and Jesters in Literature, Art, and History: A Bio-Bibliographical Sourcebook*. Westport, Connecticut: Greenwood Press.

Jasper, D. (1985). *Coleridge as Poet and Religious Thinker*. Allison Park, Pennsylvania: Pickwick Publications.

Kant, I. (1995). *Kritik der Urteilskraft*. Frankfurt am Main: Suhrkamp.

Kant, I. (1999). *Kritik der reinen Vernunft*. Köln: Parkland Verlag.

Kearney, R. (1988). *The Wake of Imagination: Toward a Postmodern Culture*. Minneapolis: University of Minnesota Press.

La Caze, M. (2000). 'Analytic Imaginary'. In M. Deutscher (ed.), *Michèle Le Doeuff: Operative Philosophy and Imaginary Practice*. New York: Humanity Books, pp. 61–80.

La Caze, M. (2002). *The Analytical Imaginary*. Ithaca and London: Cornell University Press.

Le Doeuff, M. (1979). 'Operative Philosophy: Simone de Beauvoir and Existentialism'. *Ideology and Consciousness* 6, 47–57.

Le Doeuff, M. (1987). 'Ants and Women, or Philosophy without Borders'. In A. Phillips Griffiths (ed.), *Contemporary French Philosophy*. Cambridge: Cambridge University Press, pp. 41–54.

Le Doeuff, M. (1989). *The Philosophical Imaginary*. Translated by C. Gordon. London: The Athlone Press.

Le Doeuff, M. (1991). *Hipparchia's Choice: An Essay Concerning Women, Philosophy, etc.* Translated by T. Selous. Oxford, UK and Cambridge, MA: Blackwell.

Le Doeuff, M. (2003). *The Sex of Knowing*. Translated by K. Hamer and L. Code. London: Routledge.

Lee, H. (1997). *Virginia Woolf*. London: Vintage.

Levinson, J. (ed.) (2003). *Oxford Handbook of Aesthetics*. Oxford: Oxford University Press.

Lloyd, G. (2000). 'No One's Land: Australia and the Philosophical Imagination'. *Hypatia* 15-2, 26–39.

Lovibond, S. (1994). 'Feminism and the Crisis of Rationality'. *New Left Review* 207 (Sept/Oct), 72–86.

Maras, S. (2000). 'Translating Michèle Le Doeuff's Analytics'. In M. Deutscher (ed.), *Michèle Le Doeuff: Operative Philosophy and Imaginary Practice*. New York: Humanity Books, pp. 83–104.

McGill, A.C. (1968). 'Recent Discussions of Anselm's Argument'. In J. Hick and A.C. McGill (eds), *The Many-Faced Argument: Recent Studies on the Ontological Argument for the Existence of God*. London and Melbourne: Macmillan, pp. 33–110.

McMullin, E. (1996). 'Enlarging Imagination'. *Tijdschrift voor Filosofie* 58-2, 227–260.

Midgley, M. (2005). *The Owl of Minerva: A Memoir*. London and New York: Routledge.

Moi, T. (1986). 'Vive la différence'. *Women's Review of Books* no. 6.

Moi, T. (1987). 'Introduction: Feminist Thought and the Women's Movement'. In T. Moi (ed.), *French Feminist Thought: A Reader*. Oxford: Basil Blackwell, pp. 1–13.

Moi, T. (1990). *Feminist Theory and Simone De Beauvoir*. Oxford: Basil Blackwell.

Moran, D., and T. Mooney (eds.) (2006). *The Phenomenology Reader*. London and New York: Routledge.

Morris, M. (1981–1982). 'Operative Reasoning: Michèle Le Doeuff, Philosophy and Feminism'. *Ideology and Consciousness* 9, 71–101.

Mortley, R. (1991). *French Philosophers in Conversation: Levinas, Schneider, Serres, Irigaray, Le Doeuff, Derrida*. London and New York: Routledge.

Nietzsche, F. (1988a). 'Wahrheit und Lüge im aussermoralischen Sinne'. *Kritische Studienausgabe 1*. Herausgegeben von G. Colli und M. Montinari. Berlin, New York: Walter de Gruyter, pp. 873–890.

Nietzsche, F. (1988b). *Jenseits von Gut und Böse. Kritische Studienausgabe 5.* Herausgegeben von G. Colli und M. Montinari. Berlin, New York: Walter de Gruyter.

Nietzsche, F. (2001). *The Gay Science.* Edited by B. Williams, translated by J. Nauckhoff, poems translated by A. del Caro. Cambridge: Cambridge University Press.

Nussbaum, M.C. (1986b). *The Fragility of Goodness: Luck and Ethics in Greek Tragedy and Philosophy*. Cambridge: Cambridge University Press.

Nussbaum, M.C. (1990). *Love's Knowledge: Essays on Philosophy and Literature*. Oxford: Oxford University Press.

Nussbaum, M.C. (1991). *Poetic Justice: The Literary Imagination and Public Life*. Boston: Beacon Press.

Nussbaum, M.C. (1994). 'Feminists and Philosophy'. *New York Review of Books.* 20 October, 59–63.

Plato (2001). *Euthyphro, Apology, Crito, Phaedo, Phaedrus*. With an English translation by Harold North Fowler. Cambridge, Massachusetts; London: Harvard University Press.

Plato (2003). *The Republic: Books I–V.* With an English translation by Paul Shorey. Cambridge, Massachusetts; London: Harvard University Press.

Plato (2005). *Theaetetus, Sophist*. With an English translation by Harold North Fowler. Cambridge, Massachusetts; London: Harvard University Press.

Plato (2006). *The Republic: Books VI–X.* With an English translation by Paul Shorey. Cambridge, Massachusetts; London: Harvard University Press.

Rosen, R. (1983). *Plato's* Sophist: *The Drama of Original and Image.* New Haven and London: Yale University Press.

Sallis, J. (1986). *Being and Logos: The Way of the Platonic Dialogues.* Atlantic Highlands, NJ: Humanities Press International Inc.

Sanders, K. (1993). 'Michèle Le Doeuff: Reconsidering Rationality'. *Australasian Journal of Philosophy* 71–74, 425–435.

Sartre, J.-P. (1943). *Being and Nothingness: An Essay on Phenomenological Ontologie*. London: Routledge.

Sartre, J.-P. (1968). *De walging*. Utrecht: Bruna.

Schweiker, W. (1995). *Responsibility and Christian Ethics.* Cambridge: Cambridge University Press.

Scruton, R. (ed.) (1998). *Xanthippic Dialogues*. South Bend, Indiana: St. Augustine's Press.

Shakespeare, W. (1952). *King Lear*. London: Methuen.

Smart, N. (1998). *The World's Religions: Old Traditions and Modern Transformations.* Cambridge: Cambridge University Press.

Spearshott, F. (1990). 'Imagination: The Very Idea'. *The Journal of Aesthetics and Art Criticism.* 48–1, 1–8.

Stopczyk, A. (ed.) (1980). *Was Philosophen über Frauen denken.* München: Matthes & Seitz Verlag.

Strawson, P. (1971). 'Imagination and Perception'. In L. Foster and J.W. Swanson (eds), *Experience and Theory.* London: Duckworth, pp. 31–54.

Taylor, Ch. (1982). 'Responsibility for Self'. In G. Watson (ed.), *Free Will.* Oxford: Oxford University Press, pp. 111–126.

Taylor, Ch. (1989). *Sources of the Self: The Making of the Modern Identity.* Cambridge: Cambridge University Press.

Walker, M. (1993). 'Silence and Reason: Woman's Voice in Philosophy'. *Australasian Journal of Philosophy* 71–74, 400–424.

Walton, H. (2005). 'Literature and Theology: Sex in the Relationship'. In D. Bird and Y. Sherwood (eds), *Bodies in Question: Gender, Religion, Text.* Aldershot: Ashgate, pp. 131–146.

Warnock, M. (1976). *Imagination.* London: Faber and Faber.

Warnock, M. (1996). *Women Philosophers.* London: Everyman.

Warnock, M. (2000). *A Memoir: People and Places.* London: Duckworth.

Wittgenstein, L. (1984). *Tractatus logico-philosophicus; Tagebücher 1914–1926; Philosophische Untersuchungen.* Frankfurt: Suhrkamp, 1984.

Woolf, V. (1957). *A Room of One's Own.* San Diego, New York, London: Harcourt Brace Jovanovich Publishers.

Index